THE BASICS OF
EVOLUTION

CORE CONCEPTS

THE **BASICS** OF **EVOLUTION**

ANNE WANJIE, EDITOR

ROSEN
PUBLISHING®

New York

This edition published in 2014 by:

The Rosen Publishing Group, Inc.
29 East 21st Street
New York, NY 10010

Additional end matter copyright © 2014 by The Rosen Publishing
Group, Inc.

Library of Congress Cataloging-in-Publication Data

Wanjie, Anne.
The basics of evolution/Anne Wanjie.—1st ed.—New York: Rosen, © 2014
       p. cm.—(Core concepts)
Includes bibliographical references and index.
ISBN 978-1-4777-0557-5 (library binding)
1. Evolution (biology)—Juvenile literature. 2. Evolution—Juvenile
literature. I. Title.
QH367.1 .W36 2014
576.8

Manufactured in the United States of America

CPSIA Compliance Information: Batch #S13YA: For further information, contact Rosen Publishing, New York,
New York, at 1-800-237-9932.

© 2004 Brown Bear Books Ltd.

CONTENTS

CHAPTER ONE

EVOLUTION DEFINED

Evolution is the process of change in groups of creatures over time.

Species (types) of living things change over long periods of time to adapt to their environment. Biologists call this process evolution. Although it is a pillar of biological thinking today, the theory of evolution was shocking when it was first proposed since it challenged religious views of how life on Earth began.

The publication in 1859 of English naturalist Charles Darwin's (1809–1882) book *On the Origin of Species* changed biological thinking completely and had a profound influence in many other fields

Two Darwin's rheas. These flightless South American birds resemble African ostriches and Australian emus, but each of these large bird species has evolved in isolation for millions of years.

as well. Darwin suggested that the variety of life can be explained by a process called natural selection. In nature more individuals are born than survive to adulthood. Certain individuals survive because they have some advantage over the others. These individuals are more successful in breeding and passing on the advantage to their young. This process is the driving force behind evolution.

Evidence that Darwin was right is abundant. There are fossils that show the course of evolution over time in certain groups of organisms, such as horses. Evolution is also supported by studies of DNA that shed light on the common ancestry of different organisms.

GENERATING SPONTANEOUSLY

Many people attempted to explain diversity in the natural world before Darwin. A widespread belief was the theory of spontaneous generation—that species arose from matter such as decaying organic material. The appearance of maggots and mice in conditions that seemed lifeless suggested that organisms could originate from nothing.

JEAN BAPTISTE LAMARCK

Fifty years before *The Origin of Species* French naturalist Jean Baptiste Lamarck (1744–1829) developed a theory that

Barnacle geese breed in the Arctic in the summer and over winter in northern Europe. They are so named because people once believed that the birds—which arrived in the fall seemingly from nowhere and disappeared just as mysteriously in spring—hatched from barnacles along the coast.

SHEEP SELECTION

To get an idea of how selection works, imagine a farmer has some sheep, half of which are white and the rest black. Needing white rather than black wool, the farmer selects the white sheep for mating. Because the colors are inherited, he soon has a flock of mostly white sheep.

Years earlier some of the flock escaped into a local forest. Their only predators, wolves, hunted at night and often caught the conspicuous white sheep. Soon the sheep of the forest became mostly black—because of natural selection rather than selection by the farmer.

suggested that different species arose by changing from already existing ones. He thought that favorable features gained during a parent's lifetime would be passed on to offspring—an idea known as Lamarckism.

Lamarck suggested that changes in an organism's needs due to environmental changes could make body structures increase or decrease in size based on how much they were used. Lamarck's ideas were attacked during his lifetime and later proven to be false. Today, Lamarck is remembered only for his discredited theory, and Lamarckism remains a byword for poor biology. However, modern biologists who criticize Lamarck have the benefit of hindsight. Lamarck was actually a very talented naturalist who made a number of important zoological discoveries.

EVOLUTION AND CREATIONISM

Darwin's theories were at odds with the teachings of the Bible, which asserted that Earth and all the organisms on it

A fossil herring. From such fossil evidence scientists can figure out how living organisms have evolved over millions of years.

were created by God. The argument continues to this day. People who believe that all life on Earth is the work of an all-powerful being are called creationists. They do not accept evolutionary theory as fact.

HOW IS EVOLUTION STUDIED?

Today, biologists study the process of evolution in a number of different ways. Population geneticists look at the different factors that affect inheritance. Paleontologists focus on fossils and other evidence to study how organisms evolved long ago in the past. Ecologists examine how relationships between organisms and the environment they live in can affect the process of evolution. Studies like these provide crucial information for biologists. They interpret the evidence to figure out evolutionary relationships that link different species.

DARWIN'S BULLDOG

Although Charles Darwin developed the theory of natural selection, it only became accepted after vigorous defense by other scientists against the religious establishment. Thomas Huxley (1825–1895), often called "Darwin's bulldog," was the most formidable of them. Huxley is best known for an 1860 debate on evolution with Bishop Samuel Wilberforce (1806–1873). Wilberforce made a gentle joke about Huxley's ancestry. The furious Huxley replied that he would rather be descended from an ape than a bishop!

CHAPTER TWO

SUPPORT FOR EVOLUTION

Every feature of every organism on Earth provides evidence that evolution has taken place.

C harles Darwin's theory of evolution by natural selection is relatively simple, yet scientific evidence for it (especially in the light of recent genetic advances) is so powerful that it is accepted almost universally by biologists. The world is full of evidence that supports evolutionary theory. This evidence ranges from the fossils of creatures that lived many millions of years ago to the rapid changes that are now taking place in bacteria that cause diseases.

FOSSIL EVIDENCE

Fossils are the remains or traces of long-dead organisms preserved in rock. They have been collected and puzzled over for hundreds of years.

Before the 19th century fossils were explained as leftovers from the biblical flood or as parts of creatures such as unicorns or giants. By the early

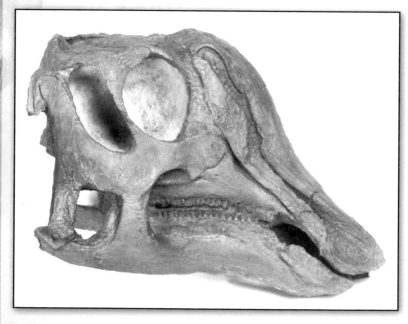

A skull of the crested duck-billed dinosaur *Lambeosaurus*, which once lived in western North America. These plant-eating dinosaurs lived between 80 and 65 million years ago. They measured from 30 to 50 feet (9 to 15m) long and were 7 feet (2.1m) tall at the hip. Fossils such as this show that many more species have lived on Earth than are alive today.

EVIDENCE IN THE ROCKS

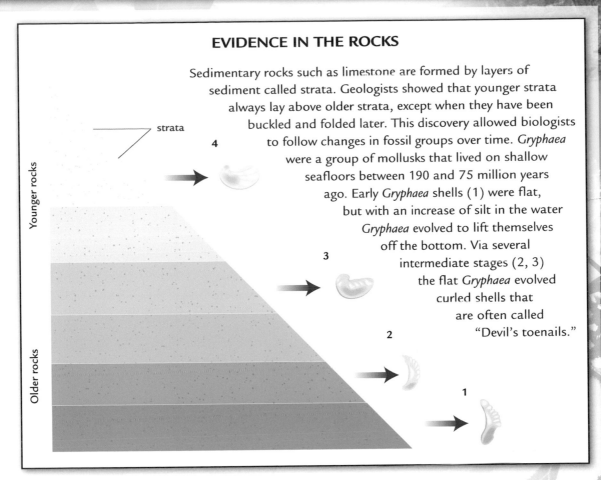

Sedimentary rocks such as limestone are formed by layers of sediment called strata. Geologists showed that younger strata always lay above older strata, except when they have been buckled and folded later. This discovery allowed biologists to follow changes in fossil groups over time. *Gryphaea* were a group of mollusks that lived on shallow seafloors between 190 and 75 million years ago. Early *Gryphaea* shells (1) were flat, but with an increase of silt in the water *Gryphaea* evolved to lift themselves off the bottom. Via several intermediate stages (2, 3) the flat *Gryphaea* evolved curled shells that are often called "Devil's toenails."

strata

Younger rocks

Older rocks

4

3

2

1

1800s biologists had begun to realize that many fossilized creatures no longer existed on Earth. They also noticed that some fossils were similar to, but not the same as, living creatures. This evidence suggested that they were distant ancestors of living animals. Geologists (people who study rocks) realized that the rocks in which fossils were found were sometimes millions of years old. These lines of evidence were in complete opposition to the teachings of the Bible, which held sway over much scientific thinking at this time.

Paleontologists (scientists who study fossils) can follow how one form of organism evolved into another over millions of years. For example, around 55 million years ago *Hyracotherium*, the earliest known horse, lived in forests in North America. It was a small, dog-sized animal with five toes on each foot. Over many millions of years animals like *Hyracotherium* evolved to become larger and lost four of the five toes. That helped them run faster. Horse evolution did not move in a straight line but more by way of a "sprawling bush." Modern horses and their relatives form the last "branch" of this bush.

Signs in the rocks also tell scientists what the environment was like—for example,

HOW FOSSILS FORM

Fossils are the preserved remains or traces, such as footprints, of living organisms that died millions of years ago. Fossilization (fossil formation) occurs in a number of steps. Bones and other hard parts of a dead organism are gradually replaced by minerals.

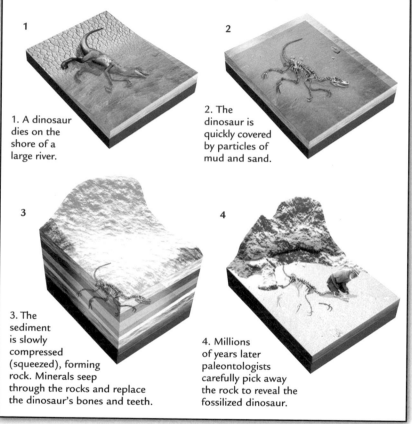

1. A dinosaur dies on the shore of a large river.

2. The dinosaur is quickly covered by particles of mud and sand.

3. The sediment is slowly compressed (squeezed), forming rock. Minerals seep through the rocks and replace the dinosaur's bones and teeth.

4. Millions of years later paleontologists carefully pick away the rock to reveal the fossilized dinosaur.

whether it was hot or cold, wet or dry. So, they can see from the fossils how living organisms have changed over time in response to major changes in the environment.

SIMILARITIES ACROSS THE GLOBE

In different parts of the world there are animals that are similar to each other but are not identical. For example, jaguars live in South America, lions in Africa, and tigers in Asia. All are big cats, but each has a different coat and forms a separate species. Evolving from a common ancestor, each big cat adapted to its environment over millions of years.

A similar pattern is found in many other creatures. For example, there are similar large, flightless birds in different parts of the world, such as the

THE SPEED OF EVOLUTION

Scientists argue about the speed at which evolution takes place. Some scientists have looked at fossils and decided there is a regular rate of change, or evolution. Others believe a theory called "punctuated equilibria" is correct. It suggests that there are long periods with no change, followed by shorter periods with very rapid change. The truth may lie somewhere between these two viewpoints.

Modern-day horses have evolved over millions of years from small forest dwellers into large, fast-running animals adapted for life on grasslands.

rhea in South America, the ostrich in Africa, and the emu in Australia. However, some creatures that look similar do not share a common ancestor and have evolved from completely different organisms. This is called convergent evolution. For example, both whales and fish have streamlined bodies and powerful tails to drive them through water. Despite these similarities, whales are only very distantly related to fish. Each group has adapted in similar ways to the challenge of movement in water.

RELIGIOUS BELIEFS

Before Darwin's work biology in Christian countries was underpinned by a literal belief in the Bible. People thought that the Earth was created in seven days in 4004 BC, and God also created animals and plants. Evolution did not take place because God had created perfect organisms. Fossils were explained away as creatures that failed to make it onto Noah's Ark and died in the flood. Many Christians today, as well as people of other faiths, think Darwin was wrong and evolution does not exist, but instead, all creatures were created by God. This idea is called creationism, and it has some powerful advocates. Some schools, for example, are not allowed to teach evolutionary theory. However, creationism has been completely disproved by more than a century of experimental evidence.

FIND YOUR TAIL!

You do not have a tail, but you do have the remnants of one—the one that your distant ancestors used to help them swing between tree branches. Mostly you do not notice this stump of a tail. However, if you fall and land right on the bottom of your backbone, you will bang it—and it will hurt. This bone is called the coccyx. It is a type of vestigial structure.

Monkeys, such as this spider monkey, use their tails to grasp objects like branches.

GEOGRAPHICAL SPREAD

Scientists know that all the continents were once joined together but have moved apart over millions of years. That explains how groups of organisms have become isolated from each other, allowing them to evolve in different ways depending on their environment.

Evolution in isolation explains, for example, the geographical distribution of marsupial mammals. They include mammals such as koalas, kangaroos, and wombats that carry their young in pouches. Marsupials once lived all over the world, but after the appearance of placental mammals (mammals whose young develop inside the mother) marsupials were replaced in the northern hemisphere. However, by this time the southern continents had already broken away from the rest. Marsupials were able to continue to evolve unchecked in South America, Australia, and Antarctica.

Antarctic marsupials disappeared when the continent froze as it moved closer to the South Pole. A few placental mammals, such as primates, did make it across to South America, but marsupials continued to prosper. However, most disappeared around 2 million years ago. South America and North America joined again, and placental mammals flooded south.

Marsupial mammals, such as these koalas, are today found mainly in Australia and New Guinea, though marsupials once occurred around the world.

Just a few marsupials, such as the opposums, survived in the Americas. In Australia and New Guinea, though, marsupials flourished, free of competition from placental mammals until people arrived on the continent.

ANATOMICAL EVIDENCE

Anatomy is the study of the structure of organisms. Anatomists look at how an animal's bones, muscles, and organs are shaped and fit together. Biologists

FIGHTING BACTERIA

Bacteria are microscopic organisms. They cause many diseases, such as tuberculosis and cholera. In the middle of the 20th century scientists began to develop a range of drugs that killed dangerous bacteria without killing the patient. These drugs are called antibiotics. Bacteria breed very quickly, producing many generations in a day. Natural selection swiftly reinforces any adaptation that helps bacteria cope with a new drug. Such a mutation spreads quickly through the bacteria population. Drug-resistant strains of tuberculosis are now a serious threat in some cities. This is an example of evolution in action.

SPOTTING CONVERGENCE

For a long time people assumed that vultures from the Old and New Worlds were separate branches of the same group, since they looked very much alike. Genetic research has shown this to be false. The vultures live very similar lifestyles, so similar features evolved in each group. Both soar high to spot food and use their powerful beaks to tear at carrion, while their heads and necks are bald to avoid feathers matted with blood. However, New World vultures such as condors are actually close relatives of storks. This is an example of convergent evolution.

Although they look alike, a griffon vulture from Africa (left) and a California condor (right) are not close relatives. Both vultures search for and feast on carrion from large animals.

compare anatomies of different species to figure out how closely related they are. The more similar a pair of organisms are, the more likely it is that they shared a recent common ancestor from which both have since evolved.

False similarities, however, may occur as a result of convergent evolution. For example, all vertebrates (animals with backbones) share a common ancestor. The huge variety of vertebrates, including fish, amphibians, reptiles, mammals, and birds, suggests that the common ancestor must have lived a very long time ago, hundreds of millions of years in the past. By contrast, similarities between apes (chimpanzees, orangutans, gorillas, and people) include an upright posture, large brain, and a flat face. They suggest a much more recent common ancestor. Biologists think that the common ancestor of apes lived around 15 million years ago.

VESTIGIAL STRUCTURES

Many animals have features that are of little use. These are called vestigial structures, and they are the remnants of features that were useful to the animal's ancestors long ago.

For example, whales have no hind legs, but they still have the remnants of pelvic bones. In land vertebrates the hind legs fit into these bones, which are at the bottom of the spine. The presence of tiny pelvic bones in whales proves that these creatures evolved from a mammal with four legs that lived and walked on land.

Snakes like boas have a pair of tiny claws on their bodies. They are the remnants of hind legs. Unlike most vestigial structures, boa legs are still used, in mating. These claws show that snakes descended from four-legged ancestors. For a period in their evolutionary history snakes burrowed underground. During this time they lost their legs. Later snakes returned to a hunting lifestyle above ground.

GENETIC EVIDENCE

Anatomical evidence for evolution is backed up by the science of genetics. By looking at DNA—the molecule that carries every individual's genetic blueprint—scientists can figure out how closely two different species are related

Humans and the tiny fungus called yeast (top) are very different organisms. Even so, studies of their DNA have shown that they share more than 30 percent of their genes—the segments of DNA that code for inherited characteristics.

and how long ago their common ancestor lived.

The DNA of humans and chimpanzees, for example, is about 99.4 percent identical. Biologists suggest that their common ancestor lived around 5.5 million years ago.

CHAPTER THREE

WHAT IS NATURAL SELECTION?

With the publication of *On The Origin of Species* in 1859 Charles Darwin revolutionized biological thinking and research.

Evolution is driven by natural selection. This process allows favorable adaptations that aid survival to spread through a population.

Within any population (regional group of the same species) of organisms some individuals are better suited to survive and breed than others. In turn, more young of the better-adapted organisms survive. This is called natural selection. It is one of the driving forces behind evolution, which is the process of change within groups of organisms over long periods of time.

Although a number of earlier thinkers had suggested that species may change over time, English naturalist Charles Darwin (1809–1882) was the first biologist to figure out how evolution works. He looked at different groups such as barnacles and pigeons to show how natural selection takes place.

LAMARCK AND LONG NECKS

French naturalist Jean-Baptiste de Monet de Lamarck (1744–1829) was among the earliest evolutionary thinkers. He thought that use or disuse of a feature by an organism decided whether the feature was passed to young. Useful features would be handed on and others lost. A giraffe's long neck, for example, would develop from a lifetime of stretching for higher branches. However, Lamarck's ideas were disproved by later biologists.

VISITING THE GALÁPAGOS ISLANDS

In 1831 Darwin set out on the British survey ship HMS *Beagle*. During his voyage Darwin made observations of animals and plants that made him doubt the accepted view of the natural world—that species did not change over time. While visiting the Galápagos Islands, 600 miles (1,000 km) off the coast of South America, Darwin looked closely at the kinds of giant tortoises that lived there. He found that each Galápagos island had its own subspecies with distinctive features. Darwin realized that the tortoises shared a recent common ancestor but had evolved in isolation on the different islands. He knew that the young of

organisms that produce their young sexually (through fusion of sperm and egg), like tortoises and people, were not identical to their parents. Yet could these small variations lead to new species? Was the Earth old enough to allow time for such changes to take place?

Around the same time that Darwin was asking himself these questions, English geologist Charles Lyell (1797–1875) suggested that Earth was a lot older than people had previously thought—old

DARWIN'S FINCHES

While on the Galápagos Islands, Darwin collected many finches. He found that similar but different species of finches had very different beaks. Darwin wrote that "one might really fancy that...one species had been taken and modified for different ends." The finches helped Darwin develop his theory of natural selection. He realized that the finches had evolved to eat different foods, forming new species on the way.

A Galápagos giant tortoise. Sadly, three of the original 14 subspecies (local forms) of these tortoises have disappeared since Darwin visited the islands, and of another subspecies only one individual remains.

AMAZING TAILS

A male peacock's tail does not help the bird survive. It is more of a hindrance that increases its chances of being caught by a predator. However, peacock tails evolved because the females favor males with the biggest, brightest tails. This is called sexual selection. Males with the best tails will produce the most young. Sexual selection drives the evolution of sexual dimorphism (differences between males and females).

enough for complex organisms to appear through evolution. Armed with this crucial information, Darwin started to develop his theory of natural selection.

ON THE ORIGIN OF SPECIES

Darwin spent around 20 years gathering evidence to support his ideas. He was eventually forced to publish his results because another English naturalist, Alfred Russel Wallace (1823–1913), had independently arrived at the same conclusions. In 1859 Darwin's *On the Origin of Species* was finally published. Darwin suggested that since more individual organisms are produced than survive, there must be a constant struggle for existence.

Creatures that are better adapted to their environment are more likely to survive, so those that possess characters giving them any advantage over others are

A SELECTIVE DISASTER

Over thousands of generations male Irish elk evolved to have antlers of enormous size. This may have been due to sexual selection by female Irish elk. Females chose the males with the largest antlers to breed with, driving the evolution of ever-larger antlers. However, this may also have led to the Irish elk's downfall. With a change in plant species over the elks' range at the end of the last Ice Age it became more and more difficult to find the nutrients needed to grow such massive antlers. By around 10,000 years ago the Irish elk was extinct.

more successful. These adaptations will increase in the population as parents produce offspring similar to themselves.

Darwin had a problem, however. He was unable to explain how features were inherited through the generations. He

A NATURAL DIVISION

White-bark pines found in such places as the Sierra Nevada Mountains occur in two forms. At high levels, where conditions are harsh, they form low bushes. On the lower slopes, which are mild and sheltered, they grow into trees. At present the two types can interbreed, but the hybrids (young produced by the breeding of tree with shrub) are less able to survive than either trees or bushes. What do you think might happen in the future?

THE MONK AND THE PEA PLANTS

Although biologists knew nothing of his work until after his death, Austrian monk Gregor Mendel (1822–1884) is today remembered as one of the most important 19th-century biologists. Experimenting with pea plants, Mendel studied simple traits such as flower color. He found that parent peas pass hereditary factors (now called genes) to their young, with half provided by each parent. Mendel realized that he could predict the proportions of the traits in the young peas.

suggested they "blended," like mixtures of paint. Critics pointed out that if this were the case, good adaptations would be quickly diluted out. Darwin was eventually proven wrong on this point. The work of Gregor Mendel showed how inheritance took place. This showed how natural selection could occur, although Mendel's work was ignored by biologists until long after Darwin's death.

FOLLOWING DARWIN

It took many years of heated debate before biologists accepted that populations evolve over time through natural selection, and that species originate by splitting from other species. Evolutionary theory was based on fossils, on biogeography (where different creatures live in the world), and the development and structure of organisms.

SURVIVAL OF THE FITTEST

This simple project shows the principles of natural selection at work. Make around 20 pea-sized balls of dough. Color half red and half green with confectionary dyes. Put all your dough balls on a green piece of paper, and put it onto a bird feeder. Investigating birds will find and eat the red balls first. That is because the green balls are similar in color to the paper, while the red ones are more visible. In effect, the green balls are better adapted to survive and are less likely to be eaten Blending into the background like this is called camouflage.

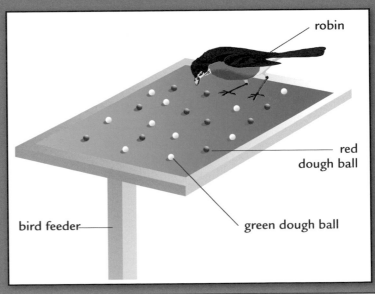

robin

red dough ball

bird feeder

green dough ball

Over recent years these branches of evidence have been enhanced by molecular biology and genetic research.

Although he himself did not coin the phrase, "survival of the fittest" provides a neat summary of Darwin's ideas. Fitness refers to an organism's ability to survive. However, if the organism fails to produce offspring that also survive and breed, advantageous adaptations are not passed on. As a result, fitness is now measured in terms of the number of offspring that survive to adulthood produced by an individual organism.

INHERITED VARIATIONS

Inherited variations are now accepted as the raw material on which natural selection acts. More importantly, biologists now understand how these variations occur and are inherited by offspring. Mutations are tiny mistakes that occur when genetic information is being copied before offspring are produced. Mutations are the source of new variation. Mutations occur at random and are unrelated to the environment in which an organism lives, but they can be of major significance in evolutionary terms. An accumulation of mutations over long periods of time can lead to the formation of a new species.

LEOPARDS AND PANTHERS

Although they look different, panthers actually belong to the same species as leopards. To understand why, biologists need to study how genes are inherited. Cubs are only born black if they inherit a copy of the black coat gene from each parent. This is a rare event; but imagine if conditions changed, and having a black coat became an advantage. The number of panthers would increase through natural selection. Over time leopards with normal coats would become the rarer of the two forms.

SELECTION SHORTCUTS

Farmers have known for thousands of years how to shortcut natural selection. By using the cattle that provided the most meat for breeding, for example, they could produce a herd of cows that gave a bumper meat yield. This is called artificial selection, and it led to the creation of the many breeds of animals and plants seen today. Features that would hinder survival in the wild could also be selected for. A bulldog, for example, is a relatively slow runner with short legs.

NICHES AND ADAPTATION

No organism can live everywhere on Earth. Each is adapted to its own niche, a specific place or role in an ecosystem, in different ways. An adaptation is a feature that helps an organism survive in its environment. Most adaptations have a genetic basis and can be inherited by future generations. However, many animals have behavioral adaptations, such as macaque monkeys that wash dirty rice before they eat it. These behaviors are learned and passed down through the generations, and are examples of nongenetic adaptations.

Understanding how adaptations work can be important when trying to figure out the ways that ancient life forms looked and acted. For example, by looking at their

UPDATING DARWINISM

During the 20th century biologists subtly revised Darwin's theory of natural selection. They refined it in light of advances in other biological fields. This update of Darwin's theory is called neo-Darwinism. Neo-Darwinism accepts that evolution has occurred and is directed by natural selection, but it incorporates evidence from genetic research, such as the importance of mutations. Neo-Darwinism also acknowledges the influence that factors other than natural selection can have on evolution, such as genetic drift.

bones, biologists have discovered how saber-toothed cats, a group that became extinct around 11,000 years ago, caught their prey. One group of saber-tooths, called scimitar cats, had long legs and short

Leopards are usually yellow-brown with a distinctive pattern of swirls and spots, like this one. Only rarely will a panther cub be born.

MORE THAN ENOUGH OFFSPRING

A female mouse can breed twice each year and produces around six offspring each time. Imagine if all the offspring of this mouse and all subsequent generations survived and had young at a similar rate. Within just 10 years the descendants of the first mouse would number more than 60 billion! The world would soon be carpeted with mice. Why do you think that does not happen?

Mice produce lots of young in their lives. Why is the world not filled with mice?

canine teeth. These cats were adapted for pursuit of small prey, such as antelope. The other group, called dirk-toothed cats, had much shorter, more powerful legs and extremely long canine teeth.

Dirk-toothed cats were adapted for ambush; they used their teeth to cause a massive injury either at the throat or in the belly. The victim quickly bled to death. In this way dirk-toothed cats could kill very large animals.

FORM AND FUNCTION

Sometimes organisms possess adaptations with an obvious function. For example, the limbs of whales and seals have evolved into flippers, which are much more efficient for moving through water than the land-adapted limbs of their ancestors. Can you think of any other adaptations these mammals have for living in water?

PHYSIOLOGICAL ADAPTATIONS

Some adaptations, such as hibernation, involve internal metabolic (energy-supply) processes. Animals like bats hibernate to survive the winter, when temperatures drop and food is scarce. They build up reserves of fat in fall and then enter a state of torpor (inactivity) in winter. During hibernation a bat's body temperature drops, its heart rate slows, and the need for energy falls dramatically. The bat wakes in spring, when it feeds as quickly as it can to replenish its fat reserves before breeding. Can you think of any other animals that hibernate?

CAT ADAPTATIONS

Look for adaptations for a predatory (hunting) lifestyle in your pet cat. You will see it has sharp teeth because it is a meat eater that must hunt and kill prey. It can retract its claws, allowing it to move quietly when stalking, but it can extend them to grab prey.

Both your domestic cat and a lion have sharp canine teeth for killing prey.

HOW DIVERSITY ARISES

If a small population of creatures moves to a new area, adaptations to the new environment will arise through natural selection. In time the group may differ sufficiently from the parent population to be classed as a new species. In this way natural selection is responsible for the tremendous diversity of life on Earth.

RECONSTRUCTING THE MOA

In 1839 English anatomist Richard Owen (1804–1892) published an accurate reconstruction of the moa, an extinct animal from New Zealand. Owen only had a fragment of limb bone to work with. How did he do it?

Owen looked closely at adaptations. Bird bone has a unique internal structure to give lightness in flight, so he knew the creature was a bird. The thickness of the bone suggested it belonged to a long-legged running bird like an ostrich. Using such observations, Owen was able to reconstruct the moa.

Owen with the bone fragment and a complete moa skeleton discovered after he showed that these animals were birds.

PREADAPTATION

Sometimes organisms carry genetic adaptations that allow them to move into a new niche without requiring further evolution. Such organisms are said to be preadapted. For example, weeds quickly colonize cleared ground because they are preadapted to that environment. They do not need to evolve further to occupy the new habitat. Next time you pass a vacant lot or neglected space, look out for these opportunistic plants.

CHAPTER FOUR

UNDERSTANDING GENETICS AND EVOLUTION

Since Darwin's time biologists have looked at how genes influence variation and evolution in the natural world.

Although biologists have shown that evolution can occur through natural selection, it is not the only cause of change in groups of organisms over time. Evolution can also result from random changes in the genetic composition of a population, a process called genetic drift, while new genes may enter a population through migration from other areas. For evolution

These early 20th-century immigrants brought genetic variety to North America.

TYPES OF VARIATIONS

Genes make us what we are. They control the way cells develop and function. Each of the genes inside the cells in your body is composed of a pair of alleles, with one allele provided by each parent. There are two main types of alleles. Dominant alleles are always expressed regardless of what the other allele in a gene is. For example, the allele for brown eyes is dominant. People with blue eyes have a pair of alleles of a different type, called recessive alleles. Blue eyes occur only in the absence of any dominant brown-eye alleles. Some features, such as height, are known as polygenic traits. They are controlled by more than just one gene. Height, for example, is partly determined by specific height genes from parents; but other genes, such as those that control growth hormones, are also important. Height is also influenced by nongenetic factors, such as diet during childhood, and whether or not the mother smoked while she was pregnant.

Height is influenced by many different genes, but environmental factors such as childhood diet are also important.

to take place, there must be a genetic basis to variations so changes that occur in one generation can be inherited by the next.

In Charles Darwin's time the way in which features were inherited was not understood. Even Gregor Mendel, who showed how characteristics were inherited, could refer only to "particles of inheritance." These "particles" were later understood to be genes. Genes form a code that drives the way cells develop.

Genes are composed of deoxyribonucleic acid, or DNA. Genes are passed

SEEING GENES

In 1910 U.S. scientist Thomas Morgan (1866–1945) used the fruit fly *Drosophila melanogaster* to study the structure of chromosomes. *Drosophila* are easy to breed in the laboratory. Their salivary glands contain just a few giant chromosomes. They can be observed easily because of their large size. Morgan discovered that banding patterns, which can be seen clearly on the chromosomes, correspond to individual clusters of genes. Why do you think this is important?

A tiny *Drosophila melanogaster* fruit fly.

from parents to young, and so are inherited through the generations.

Long, coiled-up chains of DNA called chromosomes contain sequences of genes. In animals and plants chromosomes are found in the cell nucleus.

By the end of the 19th century people had observed meiosis, the process by which sex cells (eggs and sperm) that contain half the number of chromosomes of other cells are formed. However, it was not until the early 20th century that biologists realized that variation is controlled by genes.

THE GENE POOL

The variety of genes in a population (group of organisms) can differ greatly, although larger populations are usually more diverse. The total variation of genes is called the gene pool. A gene pool can shrink dramatically should a population become very small. It may lose further diversity through genetic drift. Diversity can recover through migration, but new variation can only be created by mutations.

WHAT IS A MUTATION?

A mutation is a sudden, permanent change in the genetic material of a cell. Many mutations are negative. They increase the chances of the individual dying before it can have young, and these negative mutations do not spread through the gene pool. Some mutations are positive. They help the individual survive and breed, and quickly spread through the gene pool.

Most mutations are termed neutral—they do not harm or help the individual in any way. However, imagine if conditions change, and the environment becomes much colder or hotter, or wetter or drier. These changes might make a neutral mutation become either advantageous or disadvantageous. Those individuals that share this once-neutral mutation will prosper or suffer accordingly.

MENDEL AND DARWIN

There is no evidence that Darwin ever saw Mendel's work. Darwin's idea of inheritance was based on a blending of characteristics, not "particles," as Mendel thought. This was a major flaw in Darwin's theory of natural selection, because blending would suggest that all variation disappears over time. Darwin could not explain this part of his theory because at that time nothing was known about DNA, or the genes that determine the way characteristics are passed on to future generations.

MUTATIONS AND DNA

To understand how mutations arise, scientists had to unravel the mystery of DNA, the molecule that forms the genetic code. Success came in 1953 when English scientists James Watson and Francis Crick discovered that DNA has a double helix structure. It is a little like a spiral staircase, with each "step" made of one of four chemical compounds called bases. Each base always pairs with just one of the other three bases. When DNA replicates (copies itself) during cell division, mistakes can occur. They are mutations. Mutations occur at a faster rate when DNA is bombarded with ultraviolet radiation or comes into contact with certain types of chemicals.

Mutations help drive the process of evolution. They provide genetic variation

DNA PIONEERS

English scientists Francis Crick (born 1916) and James Watson (born 1928) won a Nobel Prize for their research into the structure of DNA, but they were not alone in working on the problem. Fellow English researcher Rosalind Franklin (1920–1958) used X-rays to figure out the shape of molecules. Her work with DNA provided Crick and Watson with vital information about the molecule's structure.

Franklin died without receiving the recognition she deserved, since her contribution to this major scientific discovery was, until recently, ignored.

Franklin peers through a microscope in a laboratory.

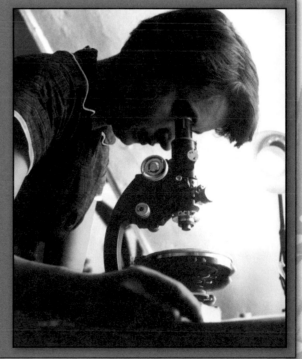

on which natural selection, the process of survival and reproduction of organisms best suited to their environment, can act to produce change.

WHAT IS DNA FINGERPRINTING?

Scientists study DNA to examine the relationships between different types of organisms using a technique called DNA fingerprinting. DNA is extracted from samples taken from the organisms and compared. Similarities between the DNA suggest a close evolutionary relationship between the organisms, while differences suggest a more distant relationship.

The degree of difference between the DNA samples also provides a good

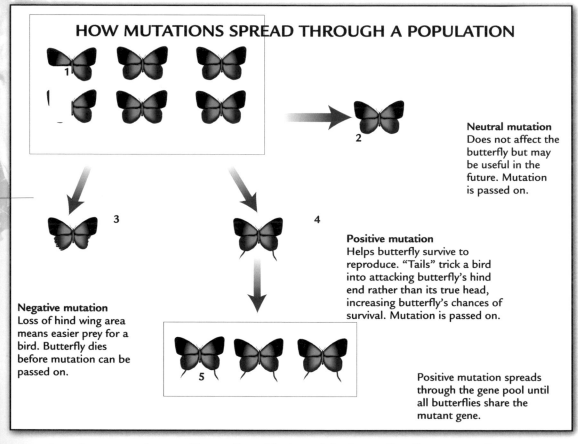

HOW MUTATIONS SPREAD THROUGH A POPULATION

Neutral mutation
Does not affect the butterfly but may be useful in the future. Mutation is passed on.

Positive mutation
Helps butterfly survive to reproduce. "Tails" trick a bird into attacking butterfly's hind end rather than its true head, increasing butterfly's chances of survival. Mutation is passed on.

Negative mutation
Loss of hind wing area means easier prey for a bird. Butterfly dies before mutation can be passed on.

Positive mutation spreads through the gene pool until all butterflies share the mutant gene.

Imagine a large population of butterflies (1). One of the butterflies has a neutral mutation (2) that is passed on, although it will not spread through the gene pool unless it becomes advantageous. Another has a negative mutation (3), which reduces its chances of survival. A third butterfly has a positive mutation (4) that increases its survival chances. This mutation spreads through the population (5).

INHERITED MEDICAL DISORDERS

Scientists' current knowledge of medical disorders enables them to pinpoint conditions that are inherited by children from their parents, such as certain heart problems. Couples from families in which such conditions have occurred previously can be tested. By looking at their genetic makeup, scientists can figure out the likelihood of such disorders being passed on to their children.

estimate of the time that has passed since the common ancestor of two different creatures was alive. When a species splits to form two new species, each new species builds up genetic differences through mutation. Scientists have a good idea of how often these changes occur. That allows them to figure out roughly how long has passed since the two species diverged.

Researchers are now using DNA fingerprinting to investigate the origins of life itself. They compare segments of DNA from very different organisms, such as humans and single-celled creatures like bacteria and protists.

CATCHING CRIMINALS

Police now use DNA fingerprinting in court as evidence against criminals. DNA can be collected from body fluids such as blood, urine, or saliva. DNA may be traceable as bloodstains on clothing, for example, for a considerable time after a crime has been committed.

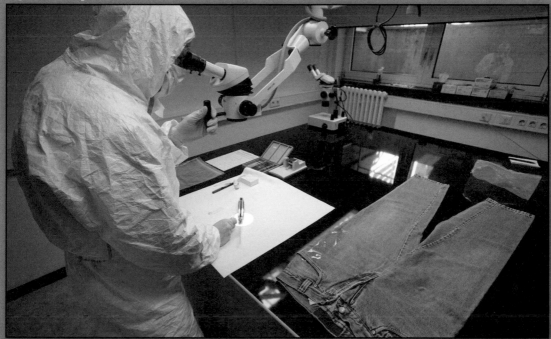

CHAPTER FIVE

UNDERSTANDING POPULATION GENETICS

Population genetics looks at the effects of genes on the features of groups of organisms, and how and why their genetic makeup changes over time.

Although there can often be amazing similarities between members of a family group, only rarely are any two exactly the same. Offspring share certain characteristics with their parents,

Children can look strikingly similar to their parents, sisters, and brothers, and sometimes even their grandparents. That is because they all share common genes.

sisters, and brothers because they are all part of the same gene pool. That is, a proportion of their genes are the same.

Young may even resemble grandparents or more distant relatives. However, each offspring is unique owing to differences in its genetic makeup. The cells of any one individual have many thousands of different genes. Sometimes a particular gene controls a specific trait, such as eye color. But the situation is often much more complicated because many genes can work together on one trait.

Each gene can exist in a variety of different forms called alleles. Some alleles are dominant. They appear frequently in a group of organisms, and the properties they code for are always expressed. Other alleles are recessive. They are rare and are expressed only when there are no dominant alleles present.

Members of the same family group have the same sets of genes. However, they are likely to carry different combinations of alleles. These combinations make us differ from one another.

SEXUAL REPRODUCTION

When a new generation of offspring is produced, sexual reproduction results in a mixing of the different alleles. This allows entirely new

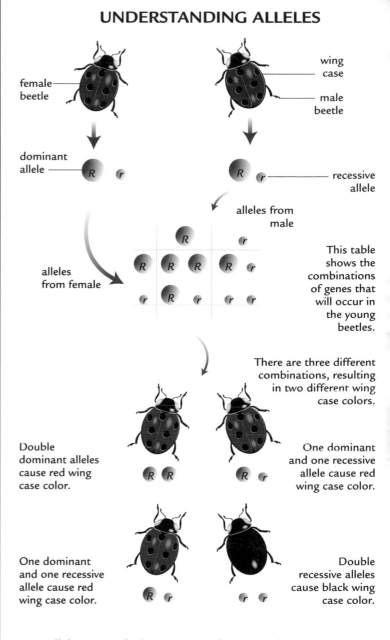

UNDERSTANDING ALLELES

female beetle · wing case · male beetle

dominant allele — R r

R r — recessive allele

alleles from male

alleles from female

This table shows the combinations of genes that will occur in the young beetles.

There are three different combinations, resulting in two different wing case colors.

Double dominant alleles cause red wing case color.
R R

One dominant and one recessive allele cause red wing case color.
R r

One dominant and one recessive allele cause red wing case color.
R r

Double recessive alleles cause black wing case color.
r r

Two alleles control wing case color in these beetles. One is dominant (R) and gives a red color; the other is recessive (r) and gives a black color. Only when an individual has two copies of the r allele does it have black wing cases.

MULTIPLE BIRTHS

In most cases of twins the offspring develop separately, may be of either sex, and are no more similar at birth than ordinary sisters and brothers. However, there are rare occasions when, owing to the division of a single zygote (fertilized egg), each of the halves grows into a separate baby. These babies are genetically identical. They are of the same sex and similar in appearance and behavior. What do people call this type of twins?

Humans usually produce only one baby at a time, but sometimes twins are born.

combinations to be produced. This process, recombination, is caused in part by the effects of meiosis, a type of cell division in which sex cells (sperm and eggs) form. Fertilization, the fusion of a male and female sex cell, is also important. Each sex cell carries inside it half of the alleles of the future offspring.

Any population is made up of a number of breeding individuals. If the process of sexual reproduction shuffles the alleles each time, then the combinations of alleles across the whole population are also likely to change. This change in the genetic makeup at population level—from one generation to another—is the basis of evolution. Evolution is the process of change that takes place as organisms adapt to their environment.

Since the characteristics of organisms are determined largely by the genes they carry, evolution can bring about changes in the characteristics of populations through the generations. There are

SELECTING SPARROWS

In 1889 a fierce storm in the United States killed a number of house sparrows. The dead sparrows were found to be long- and short-winged individuals. Intermediate-winged sparrows survived. In this case selection favored average individuals. Which type of selection is operating here? Why has natural selection acted against the extreme forms of sparrows in this situation?

several different ways in which these evolutionary changes can take place. They include mutation, natural and sexual selection, genetic drift, and migration.

NEW GENES

A mistake made when genes are replicated that leads to the appearance of entirely new genes is called a mutation. If the error in copying occurs when the sex cells are being formed, the mistake is inherited by the offspring. The variety of alleles is the result of genetic mutations. Natural selection, genetic drift, and migration change the combinations of genes in a population, but they cannot create new ones. Mutations can be positive (and increase through the population), negative (and die out), or neutral (have no effect unless conditions change).

NATURAL SELECTION

Natural selection is a process by which those individuals in a population best adapted to an environment reproduce successfully, while those that are less able fail to do so. As a result, the population changes over time—it evolves. There are three forms of natural selection: directional, stabilizing, and disruptive. Directional selection favors more extreme forms of a feature. Individuals with extreme characteristics are more likely to survive than those with more average features. Selection can sometimes be stabilizing, favoring intermediate forms at the expense of extreme types.

Selection is described as disruptive when both extremes of a trait, such as the largest and smallest, survive at the expense of intermediates. This may occur during the formation of a new species. However, selection can occur only if variation between individuals has a genetic basis and can be inherited by young.

PROBLEMS WITH SMALLER GENE POOLS

The Old Order Amish people of Pennsylvania are descended from a small immigrant population that arrived in the United States during the late 1700s. Descendants exhibit a much higher than average occurrence of several medical conditions, including polydactyly—having extra fingers and sometimes extra toes. This inherited condition is concentrated in the Amish population because they marry within their own community. Their gene pool is small compared to that of the U.S. population as a whole, so the chances of a baby inheriting recessive alleles that cause genetic disorders are much higher.

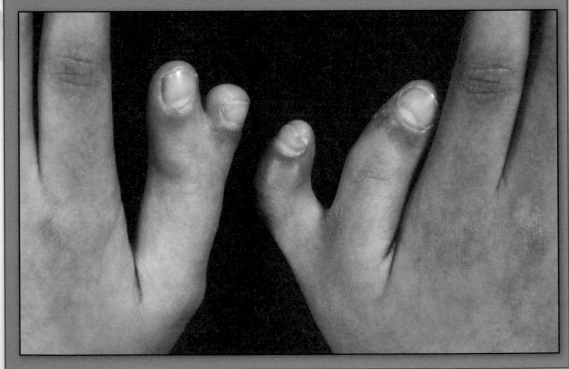

GENETIC DRIFT EXPLAINED

There is another source of genetic variation that can occur during the production of sex cells. This process, genetic drift, is a change in how often alleles appear in a population through random chance. Genetic drift is not affected by natural selection, but it can still lead to evolutionary change. In large, stable populations the effects of genetic drift tend to be canceled out by the size of the gene pool—allele frequencies may vary a little but will tend to remain the same. However, the effects of chance are more apparent in smaller populations. In a small population new generations are likely to have less genetic diversity than

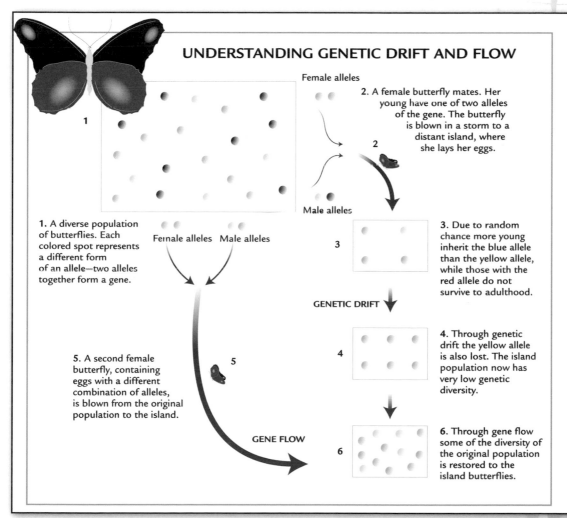

UNDERSTANDING GENETIC DRIFT AND FLOW

Female alleles

1. A diverse population of butterflies. Each colored spot represents a different form of an allele—two alleles together form a gene.

Female alleles   Male alleles

Male alleles

2. A female butterfly mates. Her young have one of two alleles of the gene. The butterfly is blown in a storm to a distant island, where she lays her eggs.

3. Due to random chance more young inherit the blue allele than the yellow allele, while those with the red allele do not survive to adulthood.

GENETIC DRIFT

4. Through genetic drift the yellow allele is also lost. The island population now has very low genetic diversity.

5. A second female butterfly, containing eggs with a different combination of alleles, is blown from the original population to the island.

GENE FLOW

6. Through gene flow some of the diversity of the original population is restored to the island butterflies.

This diagram illustrates how genetic diversity in a population can alter through two processes—gene flow and genetic drift.

ISLAND INVADERS

Remote islands, such as Hawaii and the Galápagos Islands, present ideal habitats for colonization. New arrivals are unlikely to encounter predators or competitors for resources. Their populations have little genetic diversity due to the founder effect, but despite this they stand a good chance of survival. The advantage of arriving first gives them time to adapt to their new environment over many generations, and eventually they will form new species. Which organisms do you think are more likely to reach islands before any others?

ISLAND EVOLUTION

Animals that evolve on islands often share some common features. Island birds such as kiwis are often flightless, though they had flying ancestors. With few or no predators to deal with, the birds evolved to walk and run instead. Small animals, such as tortoises, tend to become much larger on islands, while larger animals, such as deer and tigers, decrease in size to help cope with a limited food supply.

their parents. Genetic drift may result in alleles being lost. This leads to a characteristic becoming fixed. That is, both alleles that together form a gene are the same, so there is no variation. Once lost, the allele can only be reestablished through migration from elsewhere by individuals carrying the lost allele.

THE FOUNDER EFFECT PHENOMENON

Genetic drift also plays an important role in a phenomenon called the founder effect. It occurs when a small group of individuals becomes separated from the main population. This small founder group has only a fraction of the genetic variation present in the original gene pool because alleles are not spread evenly among individuals. Again, the genetic makeup of the group depends on chance. The frequency of rare alleles may be much higher in the founder group, so in future generations the rare allele may appear more frequently.

Without further mutations natural selection is also limited to variation present in the founder group. Evolution is likely to follow a different course than that of the main population. Over time this may lead to speciation—the formation of a new species.

GENE FLOW IN CONSERVATION

Reducing a habitat into small patches separated from each other can have devastating effects for the species that live there. Without gene flow genetic diversity drops. Inbreeding can cause an increase in lethal genes. Without patches of suitable habitat, or corridors, to link habitat fragments much of an area's biodiversity may be lost. Roads and highways are a major barrier to gene flow for some species. However, artificial corridors linking fragments can sometimes be set up. In some parts of Europe dormice are able to cross roads by using a network of ropes that act as corridors.

THE EFFECT OF MIGRATION

When an individual leaves one population (group of organisms of one species) and joins another, it is said to migrate. Genes carried by a migrating individual are lost from one population through emigration and gained by the population it joins through immigration. Movement of genes between populations is called gene flow.

Gene flow continues as long as the populations do not become completely separated from one another, and migrating individuals can continue to interbreed and share their genes.

GENETIC BOTTLENECKS EXPLAINED

Some species, such as the cheetah, have very little genetic variation. That is because population numbers decreased dramatically in the past. Among cheetahs this decline took place around 10,000 years ago. Cheetah numbers then recovered from a founder group, although there were no other cheetahs around. A dramatic decline in numbers with a corresponding crash in genetic diversity is called a genetic bottleneck.

SELECTION OR DRIFT?

Since it is difficult to assess genetic drift outside the laboratory, scientists have been unable to present conclusive evidence of how much variation genetic drift causes in natural populations. To find out whether a characteristic results from natural selection or drift, they must first be able to figure out whether it is adaptive (gives an advantage) or not, and for many traits this is not usually possible.

THE EFFECTS OF INBREEDING

Founder effect can cause an increase in the frequency of recessive genes that can cause serious harm to an organism. That can also happen when closely related individuals mate. The decline in fitness (ability to survive and reproduce) that results from this is called inbreeding depression. It is particularly important for organisms that can potentially breed with themselves, such as plants. Not all plants avoid inbreeding. It is a way to ensure that at least some seeds will form. However, it also leads to low genetic diversity. For most types of plants, breeding with other individuals is essential.

Turnip flowers have male parts that release pollen (dustlike particles that contain sperm) and female parts

Around 10,000 years ago cheetahs underwent a dramatic population crash—perhaps just a single female and her cubs survived. This genetic bottleneck meant that cheetahs now have very little genetic diversity.

THE HUMAN GENETIC BOTTLENECK

Cheetahs are not the only animals to have very little genetic diversity. You might be surprised to know that humans are also among the least genetically diverse of all creatures. Scientists think that is because humans almost became extinct around 70,000 years ago, perhaps due to famine or disease. The global population around this time may have fallen as low as 2,000. This collapse in numbers led to a major decrease in genetic diversity, or a bottleneck. From this low point the human population slowly began to increase. Every person alive today is a descendent of this tiny band of ancient survivors.

MINIMUM VIABLE POPULATIONS

In conserving an endangered species, scientists need to figure out the minimum viable population, or MVP. This figure is the smallest possible population that could survive, with a degree of certainty, for a set period (usually 500 years) without harmful levels of inbreeding or genetic drift. The golden lion tamarin was once one of the world's most endangered primates. Thirty years ago there were only about 100 individuals left in the wild. They live only in the Atlantic rainforests of Brazil, where their habitat has been almost totally destroyed by human activities. The MVP of this species is around 2,000. Conservationists have worked hard to establish zoo populations, and some captive-bred animals have been released into the wild.

that contain eggs. Insects carry pollen between flowers. On the outside of each turnip pollen grain are molecules called ligands. Their structure is genetically controlled. In part of the female flower called the stigma these same genes control the shape of molecules called kinases. If a pollen grain from one plant lands on a stigma of another, it grows a tube through the stigma to the eggs inside. Sperm moves through the tube to the eggs to form seeds. But if a pollen grain lands on a stigma of the same plant, the ligands on the pollen bind with the kinases. The pollen grain does not grow the tube to the eggs, and inbreeding is avoided.

EVOLUTION: GRADUAL OR RAPID?

Biologists know that evolution takes place, but at what speed? There are several main theories, but biologists are unsure which is correct. At first, it was thought that evolution was a process of gradual change. Biologists argued that small changes in an organism's structure led to a gradual

PROBLEMS WITH INBREEDING

In very small populations, breeding between closely related individuals may take place regularly. Their offspring have a good chance of inheriting harmful recessive genes. This can have a serious impact on the conservation of endangered species. Despite many years of protection from hunting, the North Atlantic right whale remains critically endangered. Individuals are less well equipped for survival due to inbreeding depression over many generations.

divergence and the formation of new species over millions of years.

Later, scientists suggested that the rate of evolution varied, and changes in the structures of fossils could be explained by rapid evolution and extreme directional natural selection. Periods with fossils of similar structures suggested times of evolutionary stability.

THE THEORY OF PUNCTUATED EQUILIBRIA

U.S. biologists Niles Eldredge (born 1943) and Stephen Jay Gould (1941–2002) proposed another model of evolution, which they called "punctuated equilibria," in

1972. They suggested that new species formed rapidly, and this speciation took place in small areas. Intermediate forms do not show up often in the fossil record as a result. These new species then move from the point of species formation and spread to new areas.

The theory of punctuated equilibria is only accepted in part by biologists today. The rate of evolution remains an issue of considerable debate.

MOLECULAR STUDIES

Scientists first estimated evolutionary rates by looking at the age of fossils and their structures. In the 1960s Japanese biologist Motoo Kimura (1924–1994) proposed the neutral theory of molecular evolution. It provided a new dating system and changed the way biologists studied evolutionary history.

Kimura suggested that most mutations are neutral—neither beneficial or harmful. Neutral mutations build up in the genome (an organism's entire genetic material) at a constant rate and spread through the population by gene flow.

Despite the genetic basis of evolution being relatively well understood for many years, scientists have only recently measured evolutionary rates using molecular studies. Before Kimura's research biologists relied on the fossil record, which is incomplete.

THE MOLECULAR CLOCK

The greater the molecular differences between two organisms, the more distantly they are related. This fact has proven an important tool in evolutionary research. However, its use for absolute dating of divergences remains controversial. It relies on the assumption that genes have mutated at the same rate over evolutionary time. There is some evidence to suggest that this may not be the case.

CHAPTER SIX

EVOLUTIONARY PATTERNS

Understanding what species are and the different ways they can form allows biologists to chart patterns in evolution over time

Populations of animals and plants alter over long periods of time through natural selection, mutation, and genetic drift. This change, or evolution, leads to a fine-tuning of an organism's adaptation to its environment. Splits in a population lead to speciation. This is the formation of a new species. The species is the basic unit of biological classification, the system used by biologists to organize their understanding of the natural world. But what exactly is a species?

WHAT IS A SPECIES?

The answer to this question may seem simple, but it is far from straightforward. The term *species* can be defined in several ways, but none encompasses all forms of life past and present. The most commonly used definition is "a group of organisms that can interbreed only with each other." This is known as the biological species concept.

There are, however, major problems with this definition. It only applies to organisms that reproduce sexually through the fusion of sperm and egg.

A clematis flower is dazzling in ultraviolet light. This evolved to attract insects, which can see this light.

COMING TO GRIPS WITH SCIENTIFIC NAMES

In 1758 Swedish naturalist Carolus Linnaeus (1707–1778) introduced a system of classification that is still used today. Linnaeus gave each species a pair of scientific names in Latin. The first, which always has a capital letter, is the name of the genus, a group of closely related organisms. Humans belong to the genus *Homo*. The second part of the name refers only to the species. In humans it is *sapiens*, so the full name is *Homo sapiens*. This system of classification allows biologists to understand the evolutionary history of a species, since closely related species share the same genus name.

Asexual creatures that reproduce by splitting in two, such as most bacteria, are excluded. Fossil organisms, too, do not fall within this definition of a species.

Also, breedings between different species do sometimes occur in nature. The young of such breedings are called hybrids. They are often sterile and unable to successfully reproduce; but for some groups, such as certain plants, hybridization can be a vital step in the formation of a new species.

Today, biologists often use a different definition for the word *species*. Called the evolutionary species concept, it states that a species consists of individuals that

VIGOROUS HYBRIDS

The existence of hybrids creates big problems for the biological species concept. Most hybrids are poorly adapted to survive, and they are often unable to breed. But sometimes hybrids of closely related species may be better equipped to survive than either of their parents. This is called hybrid vigor, and it especially applies to plants. Many crops, such as corn, are crosses cultivated to exploit hybrid vigor.

Renowned for their strength and stubbornness, mules are sterile horse—donkey hybrids.

CRYPTIC SPECIES

Some species look, to human eyes, identical to others. They can only be distinguished by detailed behavioral or genetic studies. Biologists call them cryptic species. They seem to be surprisingly common, and may be the cause of a major underestimate of Earth's biodiversity. One of the best-known discoveries of a cryptic species concerned the pipistrelle bat, which lives in Europe. Bats find their way around in the dark by emitting high-pitched squeaks and listening to the echoes from their surroundings. In the 1990s a group of English biologists noticed that some pipistrelles squeaked at a higher frequency than others, although there were no anatomical differences. Following up this hunch, the biologists looked at the genes of the bats. They found that the bats actually formed two separate species. Today, the one with the higher-frequency calls is known as the soprano pipistrelle. Biologists do not, at present, precisely understand how cryptic species evolve. However, their speciation is probably sympatric.

share the same evolutionary history. This includes asexual organisms, but can be difficult to extend to fossil groups.

THE FORMATION OF NEW SPECIES

Species arise when an existing species diverges. This can happen in different ways. One process, called allopatric speciation, takes place when a population is split by a geographical barrier. The barrier may be a river or a mountain chain. Allopatric speciation also occurs when organisms reach an off-shore island and are separated from the rest of the population.

During allopatric speciation the two populations evolve until individuals from one are unable to breed with individuals from the other. A different type of speciation, sympatric speciation, does not require geographical barriers. It occurs when a species diverges (splits) to avoid competition or make use of a new food source.

Sympatric speciation can also take place through hybridization. For many organisms a difference in the number of chromosomes (packages of genes) means breeding cannot take place between different species. This does not affect some plants, though. Instead, these species simply double up the number of chromosomes they have during reproduction. This is called polyploidy, and it results in very fast speciation that happens in a single generation. Many important crop plants, such as the potato, are polyploids.

SUBDIVIDING SPECIES

Populations within a species can differ from one another while remaining able to interbreed. These populations are called subspecies. Subspecies often occupy a particular geographic range, and they may have subtle differences of color or behavior. For example, Rothschild's giraffe lives in East Africa and can be distinguished from other giraffes by its coat color and the lack of patterning on its lower legs.

Subspecies are important when trying to understand how speciation works. They represent an intermediate stage between an ancestral population and a completely new species.

NEW CROP VARIETIES

Polyploid plants usually have fleshier leaves and larger seeds than plants with normal chromosome numbers. This is important in the production of new crop strains. *Triticum aestivum*, for example, is a type of wheat that has six times as many chromosomes as its wild ancestors.

REPRODUCTIVE ISOLATION EXPLAINED

Regardless of the mechanism, speciation depends on the individuals of one population being unable to breed with individuals from the other. Biologists call this reproductive isolation. It stops gene flow, which may act to cancel out each population's adaptations.

The barriers to reproduction may be geographical if two species become adapted to different habitats. These barriers may also be time-related. Different

SPECIATION IN ACTION

Speciation occurs when populations of organisms are isolated from one another in some way over long periods of time. Around 500 species of cichlid fish live in Lake Victoria in East Africa. Around 12,500 years ago just one or two cichlid species lived there. Their descendants diverged many times, leading to the diversity seen today. So many years may seem a long time, but this is actually an astonishingly swift speciation event.

The cichlids owe their amazing diversity to sympatric speciation. Biologists think that ancient female cichlids preferred to mate with males of certain colors. In this case the color preferences of the female cichlids provided the reproductive isolation needed for speciation to take place.

AMAZING ADAPTIVE RADIATION

Honeycreepers diverged into many new species on the Hawaiian Islands over millions of years in much the same way as the finches on the Galápagos Islands.

Through adaptive radiation the honeycreepers evolved into new niches and exploited different food sources. Their beaks changed shape dramatically to suit their foods. Take a look at the birds below and see if you can guess how each one feeds.

Most species of honeycreepers are critically endangered, and many, including the Oahu akepa, are thought to be extinct.

The way a bird feeds is closely related to the shape of its beak. The akiapola'au (*top center*), for example, gleans insects from tree trunks and leaves, and uses its long curved beak to probe crevices in the bark. A Maui parrotbill (*third clockwise from top*), on the other hand, splits dry branches with its beak to get at insects inside.

species may be active at different times of day, or they may breed at different times of the year. This is the case for many species of plants.

After speciation has taken place, mechanisms remain to help avoid breeding between members of the two species. That is because any young produced

RADIATION AND REPLACEMENT

On rare occasions during Earth's history a group has evolved a dramatic evolutionary advantage that allowed it to sweep away the competition. One of these episodes was the evolution of the amniote egg in an ancient amphibian group around 300 million years ago. Amniote eggs had waterproof shells. They allowed the animals to lay eggs far from water. Allied with a waterproof skin, the amniote egg allowed this new animal group, the reptiles, to move into niches that were unavailable to amphibians. This triggered rapid speciation through adaptive radiation. With their better adaptations for life away from water reptiles soon replaced amphibians as the dominant land vertebrates. Later reptiles diverged into two other major amniote groups, mammals and birds.

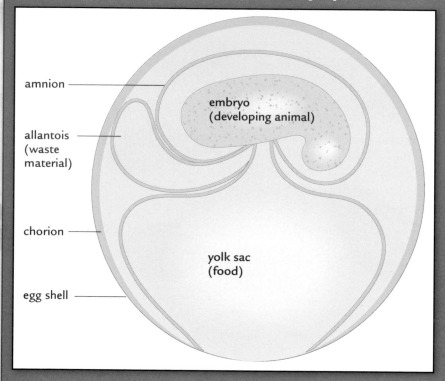

amnion

embryo
(developing animal)

allantois
(waste
material)

chorion

yolk sac
(food)

egg shell

The structure of an amniote egg, as found today in reptiles, birds, and a few mammals. The amnion and chorion are membranes that control the movement of water and oxygen. People and most other mammals have a modified form of this egg inside the uterus.

would be hybrids, which are usually less well adapted to the environment than either parent species.

ADAPTIVE RADIATION EXPLAINED

Within any environment are many niches. They are the different lifestyles and habitats of organisms. The akiapola'au, for example, fills the niche of insect catcher on Hawaiian trees. A species in an area with vacant niches will diverge to fill them. Each generation will become better adapted to a particular niche, and new species form. Biologists call this process adaptive radiation.

EATING ANTS AND TERMITES

There are many mammals that feed on ants and termites. Some have developed long noses and tongues to smell out and gather up the insects, and have powerful front limbs to tear open the insects' nests. The aardvark from South Africa is one such animal. Can you think of another animal from another part of the world that has developed the same sort of adaptations to its lifestyle?

An aardvark roams in Kenya.

The Galápagos Islands in the Pacific Ocean are well known for their 14 species of finches. These finches share a common ancestor that flew to the islands from South America. In the absence of competitors the finches radiated, and new species swiftly formed. Each finch species evolved a different beak shape. These shapes were related to the niches and food sources to which each new species was adapted.

SPECIES THAT COEVOLVE

Sometimes the evolution of two or more species is closely tied together. This is called coevolution. Some organisms have evolved such a close relationship with one another that they cannot exist in isolation. Ruminants include animals such as cattle, sheep, goats, and deer. They are unable to digest cellulose, a tough chemical found in plant material, but ruminants need the energy it contains.

Ruminants are dependent on millions of microorganisms that live in their guts. The microorganisms break down the cellulose. In return, the ruminants provide a safe, warm environment with unlimited food for their tiny internal partners. Neither the ruminants nor the microorganisms could survive without the other. A close relationship like this, in which both partners benefit, is called a mutualism. It results from millions of years of coevolution.

PARASITES AND SEX

Animals coevolve with their parasites. Biologists think that sexual reproduction, when sperm fuses with an egg, evolved as part of an "arms race" with parasites. Sexual reproduction allows a faster evolutionary response than asexual forms of reproduction, such as budding, since genes recombine to produce new genetic combinations.

However, coevolution does not always result in mutual benefit. For example, predators and their prey are involved in a biological "arms race" As predators evolve and become increasingly successful at hunting, their prey also evolve better ways of escaping capture.

CONVERGENT EVOLUTION AMONG ORGANISMS

Organisms that are not closely related can evolve similar anatomies in response to similar environments. This is called convergent evolution.

Many Australian marsupials are convergent with mammals from other parts of the world. For example, there is a burrowing marsupial that looks just like a mole. There is a gliding marsupial that is very similar to a flying squirrel, and even a marsupial "cat," the quoll, that looks and acts like a domestic cat.

JOIN THE ARMS RACE

In order to survive, prey animals have developed a wide range of adaptations that help them locate and escape from predatory animals. Ungulates, for example, are hoofed mammals, many of which are plant eaters that live on grasslands.

Most ungulates live in herds. That is because many eyes are better at spotting potential predators than just a single pair. Can you think of any other antipredator adaptations that these animals share?

Sheep are ungulates that live in herds.

ITERATIVE EVOLUTION

Convergent evolution does not have to take place at the same time. Study of the fossil record shows that certain body patterns, or ecomorphs, have evolved again and again in different animals groups. Biologists call this iterative evolution. A good example is the wide range of saber-toothed mammals.

Saber-toothed mammals used their long canine teeth to help them kill large prey quickly. The earliest saber-tooths belonged to a group of mammals called the creodonts, which lived around 50 million years ago. Later, saber teeth evolved twice among the carnivores, first in the extinct, catlike nimravids, then in the true cats themselves. The last of these saber-toothed cats, Smilodon, lived in North America and died out only around 11,000 years ago.

THE SABER-TOOTH EXAMPLE

Saber teeth also evolved among marsupial mammals. *Thylacosmilus* was a leopardlike animal that lived in South America until around 2 million years ago. Thylacosmilus had truly enormous canine teeth. These teeth rested within a pair of flanges that extended down from the lower jaw. The canines of this fearsome beast continued to grow throughout its life. The flanges helped wear the teeth down and kept them sharp.

There are no saber-toothed mammals today, but the clouded leopard from Central Asia has, relatively, the largest canines of any cat. Maybe over the next million years or so, descendants of this forest leopard will evolve true saber teeth.

WHY DO SOME SPECIES BECOME EXTINCT?

More than 99 percent of all the species that have ever existed are now extinct. The average "lifespan" of a species (time between species formation and extinction) is 2 to 3 million years, although some, such as horseshoe crabs, have changed very little over much longer periods of time.

Extinction can be caused by climate or habitat changes, the effects of competing organisms, and volcanoes or meteor impacts. At times in Earth's history large numbers of species have died out in a short space of time. Biologists call them mass extinctions. For example, a mass extinction saw the end of the dinosaurs 65 million years ago.

DEAD AS THE DODO

The dodo was a flightless relative of the pigeon. It was endemic (unique to) the island of Mauritius in the Indian Ocean. Following the discovery of the island by Dutch sailors in 1598, dodo numbers began to fall. The birds were not hunted a great deal (it was noted that dodo flesh was particularly foul tasting). However, dodos laid eggs on the ground, and their nests were vulnerable to attack by pigs, rats, and monkeys introduced by settlers. Dodos had evolved in the absence of predators and had no way of dealing with these new enemies. The birds could not breed fast enough to replace the losses, and by around 1681 the dodo was extinct. Hundreds of other island birds around the world have disappeared due to human interference over the past 500 years or so.

CHAPTER SEVEN

THE BEGINNINGS OF LIFE ON EARTH

Scientists believe the first simple life forms evolved in the oceans around 3.8 billion years ago. More than 3 billion years later plants and animals first moved from the waters onto Earth's dry land.

Around 4.5 billion years ago the newly formed Earth was a lifeless ball of molten rock. Volcanoes erupted, releasing gases and water vapor, which formed an atmosphere. It was different from the atmosphere of today, since it did not contain oxygen and was rich with poisonous gases. The water vapor gradually cooled to form the oceans, where life began around 3.8 billion years ago.

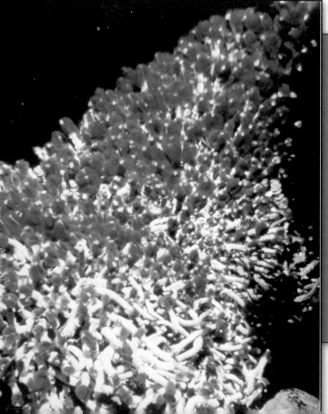

THE CRADLE OF LIFE

Biologists are divided over the type of environment in which life first appeared on Earth. Some believe life began within an ice-covered ocean. Others think it happened in the boiling cauldron of a hydrothermal vent on the seabed. Yet other experts believe that life began in shallow tidal pools fed by minerals from geysers and volcanoes. Meteors and comets that crashed onto the young Earth's surface may also have helped supply the raw materials needed before life could begin.

Tubeworms on a hydrothermal vent. Could vents like this have been the place where life on Earth began?

The earliest known life forms were tiny, single-celled organisms called prokaryotes, such as bacteria. Some, called cyanobacteria, used energy from sunlight to make food, releasing oxygen in the process. The oxygen formed a layer of ozone gas high in the sky that cut out many of the sun's harmful ultraviolet rays. The buildup of oxygen killed off many ancient prokaryote groups, but the survivors were able to use oxygen to produce energy from food efficiently.

EUKARYOTES

Around 1.8 billion years ago more advanced organisms called eukaryotes evolved. Unlike prokaryotes, these single-celled organisms had a nucleus containing genetic material. The first eukaryotes formed through the union of two different prokaryotes that lived together for mutual benefit. One of these once-free organisms now forms the mitochondria, miniorgans in cells that provide energy.

MULTI-CELLED ORGANISMS

GEOLOGICAL TIME

Biologists divide Earth's history into huge eras, which are separated into periods. The order of periods was determined by looking at the fossils contained in the rocks. By analyzing how radioactive minerals decay in rocks from each period, scientists can estimate the time (shown here in millions of years) since each period occurred.

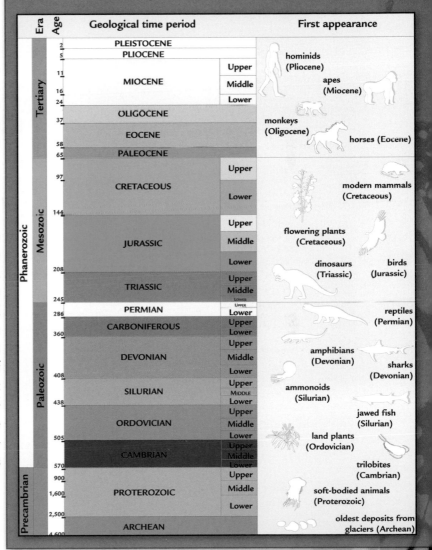

Era	Age	Geological time period		First appearance
Phanerozoic — Tertiary	2	PLEISTOCENE		hominids (Pliocene)
	5	PLIOCENE		
	11	MIOCENE	Upper	apes (Miocene)
	16		Middle	
	24		Lower	
	37	OLIGOCENE		monkeys (Oligocene)
	58	EOCENE		horses (Eocene)
	65	PALEOCENE		
Mesozoic	97	CRETACEOUS	Upper	modern mammals (Cretaceous)
	141		Lower	flowering plants (Cretaceous)
		JURASSIC	Upper	
			Middle	
	208		Lower	dinosaurs (Triassic)
	245	TRIASSIC	Upper	birds (Jurassic)
			Middle	
			Lower / Upper	
Paleozoic	286	PERMIAN	Lower	reptiles (Permian)
	360	CARBONIFEROUS	Upper	
			Lower	
		DEVONIAN	Upper	amphibians (Devonian)
			Middle	sharks (Devonian)
	408		Lower	
		SILURIAN	Upper	ammonoids (Silurian)
	438		Middle	
			Lower	jawed fish (Silurian)
		ORDOVICIAN	Upper	
	505		Middle	land plants (Ordovician)
			Lower	
		CAMBRIAN	Upper	trilobites (Cambrian)
	570		Middle	
			Lower	
Precambrian	900	PROTEROZOIC	Upper	soft-bodied animals (Proterozoic)
	1,600		Middle	
	2,500		Lower	
	4,600	ARCHEAN		oldest deposits from glaciers (Archean)

Millions of years later metazoans, organisms consisting of many cells, appeared. Cells were organized into tissues specialized for feeding, moving, and reproducing. One of the oldest

FOSSIL IMPRINTS

Ediacaran organisms are known only from the imprints that their bodies made in soft mud or trace fossils such as burrows and tracks. Experts use these clues to try to figure out what the creatures looked like. They test their theories by making models that create similar prints. You can carry out similar experiments by making imprints of natural objects such such as leaves or pine cones in wet clay. Then get your friends to try to guess what made the prints.

The imprints of many ediacaran animals look like modern jellyfish.

included worms and jellyfish. They are called ediacarans, after the Ediacara Hills in Australia, which contain a famous deposit of fossils from this time. Most of the phyla, or large groups, of animals with shells and other hard body parts appeared during a period called the Cambrian explosion, about 535 million years ago. Important groups such as the mollusks, echinoderms (starfish and relatives), and arthropods (which today include spiders and insects) appeared around this time.

EARLY VERTEBRATES

Around 450 million years ago the first vertebrates (backboned creatures) developed. They were jawless fish similar to modern lampreys. Later, in Devonian times some types of lobe-finned fish evolved lunglike pouches to breathe air and sturdy fins to heave themselves along the bottom. Fish like these began to crawl onto the shore, perhaps to escape competition with other fish or to feed. They joined plants and animals, such as insects and spiders, that had already colonized the land.

These ancient fish evolved into amphibians. Although they could move and breathe on land, they quickly lost water through their skins and had to return to water to breed. With the evolution of

metazoan fossils known is the trail left by a wormlike animal as it burrowed through the mud more than 1 billion years ago.

These ancient soft-bodied metazoans

THE BURGESS SHALE

In 1909 a rich source of Cambrian fossils was found in the Burgess Shale, high in the Rocky Mountains in Canada. These rocks date back 530 million years and contain superb fossils of a wealth of organisms, including worms, trilobites, sponges, and sea cucumbers, plus creatures that belong to completely different, long-extinct groups.

HOW MANY DIGITS?

Take a close look at your fingers. In your very distant ancestors these bones formed the rays of a fin. After these lobe-finned fish invaded the land, the rays became digits. Scientists were surprised to find that early land vertebrates had up to 8 digits rather than the 5 found today. The extra digits were lost soon after the invasion of the land. Also, check out how the bones in your arm and hand have evolved over millions of years.

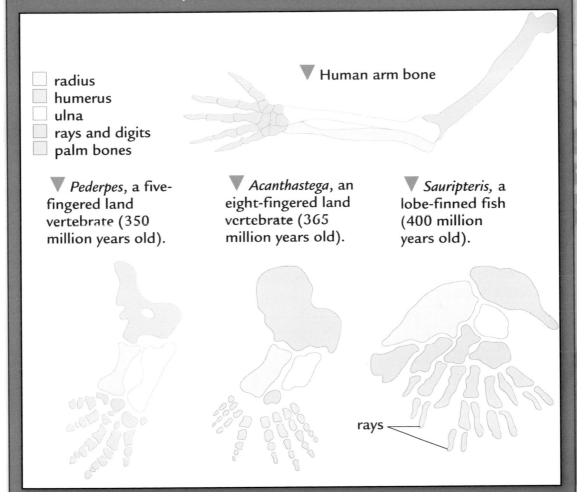

- radius
- humerus
- ulna
- rays and digits
- palm bones

▼ Human arm bone

▼ *Pederpes*, a five-fingered land vertebrate (350 million years old).

▼ *Acanthastega*, an eight-fingered land vertebrate (365 million years old).

▼ *Sauripteris*, a lobe-finned fish (400 million years old).

rays

the amniote, or shelled, egg, around 330 million years ago a new group of vertebrates with waterproof skins, the reptiles, displaced the amphibians as the main land vertebrates.

EARLY REPTILES

Since they could live and lay eggs far from water, reptiles were able to colonize many new habitats. Early reptiles looked

This salamander is an amphibian, the most ancient group of land vertebrates.

MASS EXTINCTIONS

Throughout Earth's history organisms have evolved, flourished, and died out. Sometimes vast numbers of species die out around the same time. This is called a mass extinction. The causes of mass extinctions are hard to pinpoint. Some may have been caused by asteroid impacts or volcanic eruptions that blocked out the sun.

The greatest mass extinction occurred at the end of the Permian period, 245 million years ago, when up to 95 percent of all life on Earth became extinct. Scientists think mass extinctions occur in cycles. They happen, on average, once every 26 million years.

like small lizards; but after the Permian mass extinction reptiles came to dominate the land, sea, and sky.

Marine reptiles such as the long-necked plesiosaurs, the mosasaurs, and the dolphinlike ichthyosaurs swam in the oceans along with fish, crustaceans such as crabs and lobsters, and mollusks such as ammonites and squids. Flying reptiles called pterosaurs skimmed through the air on skin-covered wings. The largest and most spectacular reptile group, the dinosaurs, lived on land along with insects, amphibians, early mammals, and birds. With the evolution of flowering plants around 100 million years ago insects flourished, and new groups such as bees appeared.

THE AGE OF DINOSAURS

More than 1,000 different dinosaur species have been identified from fossils. Some were small, chicken-sized animals, but others, such as long-necked sauropod dinosaurs like *Diplodocus*, were as big as jet liners. Biologists can tell a lot

WHY DID DINOSAURS GROW SO BIG?

Huge, plant-eating sauropod dinosaurs such as *Diplodocus* and *Brachiosaurus* were far bigger than the largest land animal of today, the African elephant. These giants evolved long necks that helped them browse among the treetops and spot danger from afar. When predatory dinosaurs also grew large, only the biggest individual sauropods survived to pass on their genes. This biological arms race drove the evolution of ever-larger sauropods, culminating in *Argentinosaurus*, which may have weighed more than 100 tons (90 metric tons)!

about how dinosaurs lived by looking at their bones. The structure of dinosaur teeth reveals that many dinosaurs, including the sauropods, stegosaurs, ankylosaurs, and ceratopsians such as *Triceratops*, ate plant material. Others were predatory meat eaters. One of the biggest and best-known, *Tyrannosaurus rex*, was a solitary hunter; but smaller, nimbler predators such as coelurosaurs are thought to have hunted in packs.

HOW DINOSAURS STAYED WARM

After many years of debate scientists are now sure that unlike living reptiles, dinosaurs were warm-blooded and did not rely on their surroundings for temperature control. Sauropods were large enough to retain their heat permanently. Smaller species produced their own heat to stay warm. Stunning fossil finds were made in China in the 1990s of dinosaurs with plumages of fine, downy feathers that kept them warm. Some pterosaurs also had hairs on their bodies to retain heat. The presence of feathers on dinosaurs resolved another long-running debate. It proved that birds, like the

WHY DID THE DINOSAURS DISAPPEAR?

Scientists disagree about why dinosaurs and other animal groups died out 65 million years ago, at the end of the Cretaceous period. Some experts believe that a giant meteor crashed into Earth off the Yucatán Peninsula in Mexico. It would have raised a cloud of dust that blotted out the sun, causing most plants to die. Others think that massive volcanic eruptions filled the air with ash and poisonous gas to similar effect. Others believe that the giant reptiles were dying out anyway because of long-term climate change. Why do you think the dinosaurs died out?

sparrows on your bird feeder, descend from dinosaurs.

THE EVOLUTION OF BIRDS

Birds evolved from small dinosaurs around 170 million years ago. The feathers that dinosaurs used to keep warm were modified for flight. The discovery in 2003 of a gliding dinosaur with four wings, one on each leg, strongly suggests that birds developed from dinosaurs adapted for climbing that glided from tree to tree. Ancient birds

DOLPHIN MIMICS

Ichthyosaurs were marine reptiles with powerful, streamlined bodies ending in a forked tail. They had two front flippers for steering and long, narrow jaws lined with sharp teeth. Unlike other reptile groups that laid eggs on land, ichthyosaurs gave birth to live young in the water. In all these ways these speedy swimmers closely resembled modern dolphins, which are marine mammals; but the two groups are only distantly related. This is an example of convergent evolution, in which different groups evolve along similar lines to suit a certain environment.

Butterflies, such as this swallowtail, evolved from moths that flew in the day to escape predation by the newly evolved bats 50 million years ago.

retained several reptilian characteristics not present in modern birds. *Archaeopteryx*, for example, had a long, bony tail, teeth, and claws on its wings.

EARLY MAMMALS

Another major vertebrate group, mammals, had evolved from reptiles slightly earlier, around 210 million years ago. Mammals developed from a group of mammal-like reptiles called cynodonts. While dinosaurs dominated the land, these warm-blooded, furry creatures remained small and ratlike.

Around 65 million years ago a mysterious disaster led to the extinction of the dinosaurs, along with the pterosaurs, most of the marine reptiles, and several other groups such as the ammonites. Smaller reptiles, such as lizards, turtles, and crocodiles, survived, along with amphibians, mammals, and birds, and invertebrate groups such as spiders and insects. The extinction of the dinosaurs allowed mammals to grow larger, and soon they became the dominant vertebrates on land and in the sea.

THE DIVERSIFICATION OF MAMMALS

On land the mammals quickly diversified. In the northern hemisphere the first horses, camels, elephants, monkeys, and rodents appeared, along with the forerunners of carnivores such as wolves, bears and cats. They were all placental mammals. Their young developed inside their mothers and were born well developed. In South America, Australia, and Antarctica a different group, the marsupials, flourished. Their young were born tiny and helpless, and developed inside a pouch on the mother's body. Just a few mammals, such as the spiny anteaters, revealed their reptile origins by continuing to lay eggs.

By around 50 million years ago bats flew in the night sky. Bats had a dramatic effect on moths and other nighttime insects. So severe was their predation that one group of moths gave up nocturnal life altogether and switched to the daytime. These insects became modern butterflies.

By the Miocene hoofed mammals such as deer and pigs thrived, while rodents diversified to become the largest of mammal groups. Being warm-blooded helped mammals survive climatic changes during the Pliocene, when long, cold periods called ice ages were interspersed with warmer spells.

FOSSIL HUNTING

The next time you head for the coast, try searching for fossils of your own. You do not need much equipment, just keen eyes and a bag to hold your finds. The best places to look are on shores near cliffs that contain sedimentary rocks, such as chalk, shales, sandstone, or limestone. A local guidebook will tell you where to find rocks like these. Study loose rocks rather than chipping away at rocks with a hammer, and keep away from dangerous cliffs. Later, you can identify your fossils with a field guide.

A woman holds up a fossilized fish.

CHAPTER EIGHT

THE EVOLUTION OF HUMANS

A skull of the humanlike creature *Australopithicus sediba*, a species that lived in southern Africa nearly 2 million years ago.

Humans started to evolve from apelike ancestors more than five million years ago. Gradually, humans became skillful tool users, invented language, and spread across the world.

Charles Darwin was the first person to hint that humans had evolved over millions of years from apelike creatures. Darwin's views caused outrage and provoked ridicule. However, most people today accept the idea of human evolution. The theory is backed up by finds of fossil bones, ancient tools, and trackways, and through analysis of human and ape DNA.

The group from which humans descend split from the ancestors of modern apes around 5.5 million years ago, although fossils found in Chad in 2002 may push this figure back to 7 million years ago. Either way, the two groups evolved along separate lines. Humans' ape ancestors lived in forest trees, probably in East Africa. Around 5 million years ago the forerunners of humans moved

DNA EVIDENCE

In recent years scientists have carried out DNA tests on humans and primates that show that people are closely related to apes such as chimpanzees and gorillas. Our closest living relatives are bonobo chimpanzees, which live in declining numbers in West Africa. This DNA evidence is supported by other scientific studies comparing the blood, brains, and other physical structures of humans, monkeys, and apes.

from the trees to the ground, perhaps after a decline in forests due to climate change. They began to walk upright, freeing their hands for other tasks.

These prehumans, which together with their human descendants are known as hominids, began to evolve bigger brains. The earliest recognizably human-like creatures lived 4 million years ago. They belong to a genus (group) called *Australopithecus*, which means "southern ape," since their fossils were first found in southern Africa.

AUSTRALOPITHECINES

Australopithecines lived in eastern and southern Africa between four and two

APELIKE ANCESTORS

The first chapters of the Bible state that God created humans in His image and set them above all other animals. In the mid-19th century Christians took these words literally, so Darwin's suggestion that humans had evolved from more primitive creatures caused an uproar. Most people thought Darwin was saying that humans were descended from monkeys, but that was a misunderstanding.

Darwin realized that humans and apes shared a common ancestor in the distant past, but that apes have also continued to evolve. However, many people at the time thought that Darwin's ideas were ridiculous.

Stone hand axes possibly used by human ancestors were found at this archaeological dig site near West Turkana in Kenya.

A FABULOUS FORGERY

Once Darwin's views became widely accepted, scientists searched hard for a "missing link." This halfway stage between apes and humans would prove that humans had evolved from apes. In 1915 an apelike human skull was found in a quarry in Piltdown, England. Piltdown Man was soon hailed as the missing link. For 40 years the authenticity of Piltdown Man was unquestioned, but tests in 1953 showed it was a hoax, made by combining human and ape remains. No one knows who carried out this famous forgery.

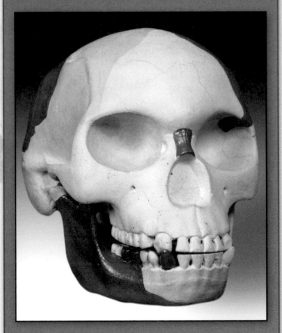

The famous Piltdown skull.

million years ago. They looked like apes, but they walked upright as they wandered the plains in search of fruit, nuts, and roots. They were smaller than modern humans, with brains about one-third the size of ours. Several different types of australopithecines have been identified so far. They include the slender, slightly built species *Australopithecus afarensis*, which was discovered in Ethiopia in 1974. The first specimen found was a female nicknamed "Lucy."

Lucy was small, less than 4 feet (120cm) tall. She had a chimp-sized brain and long, apelike arms, but she stood and walked upright. Many paleontologists think that humans are descended from a closely related species called *Australopithecus garhi*. This species was also discovered in Ethiopia in 1999.

HOMO HABILIS

By two million years ago early humanlike hominids had evolved from one of the australopithecines. The first recognizably human species, which belonged to the genus *Homo* just as modern humans do, was *Homo habilis* (meaning "handy human"). Remains of this human ancestor have been found in Kenya and Tanzania in East Africa. Studies of the fossils show that *Homo habilis* was taller than any australopithecine, with a less jutting jaw and a brain around half the size of a modern human's. "Handy humans" are so-called because they were the first to fashion rough stone tools for cutting and scraping. Animal bones found in their camps bear scratches made by the stone tools of our ancestors. No one can be sure whether these early humans actively hunted animals or simply scavenged meat from the kills of other predators.

AFRICAN FINDS

Fossils of human ancestors such as the australopithecines and *Homo habilis* come from eastern and southern Africa, where many hominid species, including our own, evolved. The rocks of the Great Rift Valley contain many vital clues about human evolution. In 1964 British paleontologists Louis (1903–1972) and Mary (1913–1996) Leakey found remains of *Homo habilis* at Olduvai Gorge in Tanzania. Many other remains were found in the gorge. Ethiopia is also rich with unique fossils. In 1974 U.S. paleontologist Don Johanson (born 1943) found a skeleton of *Australopithecus afarensis* at Hadar in Ethiopia. He named the soon-to-be-famous skeleton "Lucy."

FOOTPRINTS IN STONE

In 1976 English paleontologist Mary Leakey made an amazing discovery at Laetoli, Tanzania. She found the fossilized tracks of two ancient hominids. They had wandered across a layer of freshly fallen volcanic ash, leaving footprints that later became fossils. Paleontologists think that the 3.6-million-year-old footprints were made by a pair of australopithecines. One set of prints is much smaller than the other, suggesting that the tracks were made either by a male and a female or by an adult and a child.

STANDING UPRIGHT

By about 1.8 million years ago *Homo habilis* had evolved into several different species. Once they were lumped into a single species called *Homo erectus*, or "upright human"; but today they are split into several species, including *Homo heidelbergensis* and *Homo ergaster*. These hominids again originated in Africa but later migrated to settle in distant regions such as Europe, China, and, by around 1 million years ago, Indonesia. Erectus-like hominids were taller and faster than earlier species. Their brains increased in size over many thousands of generations until they were only a little smaller than that of modern humans. Scientists believe these early humans were the first to make fire and to fashion clothing from animal skins to help cope with harsh winter weather.

MALES AND FEMALES

There is a marked difference in size between males and females in ancient hominids such as *Homo habilis*. Males of this species reached about 5 feet (1.5m) tall, while females were only 3 to 4 feet (90 to 120cm) tall. This difference, called sexual dimorphism, is also seen in apes such as gorillas as well as many other animal species. It became less marked in hominids by about one million years ago and is only slight in modern humans.

Although there is some sexual dimorphism in modern humans, it is less marked than in our hominid ancestors.

MAKING CASTS OF TRACKS

Scientists make casts of fossilized tracks, like the prints found at Laetoli, using plaster of Paris. Try making a cast of an animal track or even your own footprint in wet mud or sand using the same technique. Make a ring of heavy paper, and put it around the print. Then mix the plaster of Paris with the water in a bowl. Pour the thick plaster of Paris mixture onto the print, wait 20 minutes, and then lift it free. When the cast is quite hard about a day later, you can clean and decorate it if you like.

THE RISE OF *HOMO SAPIENS*

By around 250,000 years ago one of these hominids (probably *Homo heidelbergensis*) had evolved into *Homo sapiens*—our own species—meaning "wise human." By 130,000 years ago modern humans, which belong to the subspecies *Homo sapiens sapiens*, had evolved in East Africa. All the people alive in the world today descend from these ancient folk.

There were other human subspecies around at this time, though. *Homo sapiens neanderthalensis*, or Neanderthal people, had short, burly bodies and lacked a chin. Neanderthals lived in Europe and the Middle East from around 130,000 years ago. They were skilled toolmakers and expert hunters—and the first people to bury their dead. Neanderthals died out around 30,000 years ago, at about the same time that *Homo sapiens sapiens* began to make rapid technological and cultural strides.

OUT OF AFRICA—THE PROOF

Homo sapiens evolved from other hominids around 250,000 years ago. A great deal of controversy has surrounded the question of where this took place. Some biologists thought that modern humans migrated from Africa recently, swiftly supplanting other humanlike hominids around the world. This is called the "Out of Africa" scenario. A separate school of thought—called multiregionalism—held that modern humans evolved many times in different places in Asia, Europe, and Africa from hominids that left Africa much earlier.

Dramatic fossil finds in 2003, however, have conclusively proven that the "Out of Africa" scenario is correct. The fossils, from Herto, Ethiopia, date from around 250,000 years ago and include the skulls of three individuals. They exhibit a blend of modern features and those found in ancestral species such as *Homo heidelbergensis*. The fossils support genetic evidence suggesting the time and place of the appearance of modern humans. Modern humans evolved in Africa and spread from there across the world.

ARE ANY MODERN PEOPLE RELATED TO NEANDERTHALS?

Neanderthals lived in Europe and Mediterranean lands until around 30,000 years ago. Short, powerful, and stocky, they were adapted for survival in cold climates. Fossils from Israel show how Neanderthals and modern humans moved in and out of the area as the climate changed over thousands of years. Although evidence from Herto shows that Neanderthals were probably not the ancestors of modern people from these areas, a remarkable fossil of a child found in 1998 in Portugal had a blend of Neanderthal and human characteristics. This possible hybrid fossil suggests that on occasions humans and Neanderthals did interbreed.

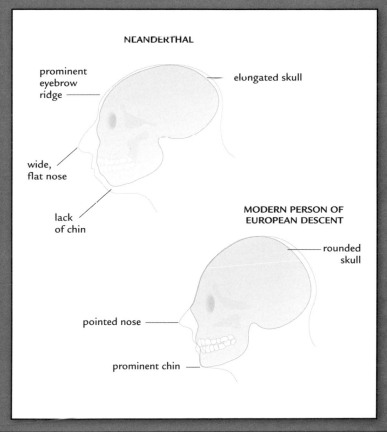

NEANDERTHAL

prominent eyebrow ridge

elongated skull

wide, flat nose

lack of chin

MODERN PERSON OF EUROPEAN DESCENT

rounded skull

pointed nose

prominent chin

THE MOTHER OF HUMANITY

Most human cells contain tiny miniorgans called mitochondria that provide energy for the cell. These miniorgans have their own DNA (separate from the DNA in the nucleus, which is inherited solely through the female line. In other words, all your mitochondrial DNA is inherited from your mother. By looking closely at this DNA, biologists have shown that everyone alive can trace their ancestry to a single female who lived around 130,000 years ago. Known as "mitochondrial Eve," this woman lived in Africa.

SPREADING AROUND THE WORLD

Around 100,000 years ago modern humans began to spread from Africa to other parts of the world. People had reached distant Australia by 60,000 years ago. By 30,000 years ago people had colonized northern Asia. Their descendants, around 14,000 years ago, crossed into North America via a land bridge through the Bering Strait. These people then

Reconstruction of paintings of bulls found in the Lascaux Cave in France. The people who created the original such paintings were modern humans. They also carved sculptures from horn, bones, and stone.

quickly spread south through Central and South America.

THE BEGINNINGS OF CIVILIZATION

Between 40,000 and 10,000 years ago a group of modern humans called Cro-Magnons lived in Europe, the Middle East, and North Africa. Around 30,000 years ago they began to advance rapidly, developing better tools for carving, cutting, and drilling. They also made needles to sew clothing and spears and harpoons to hunt animals and fish. Language helped them coordinate their hunts.

Around this time humans began to create art. Stone carvings by native Australians are among the most ancient. Later prehistoric art includes paintings of animals such as deer, horses, and bison on the walls of caves in Europe, as well as sculptures in bone, stone, and clay.

Around 11,000 years ago people in the Middle East begin to raise crops and keep domestic animals. Abandoning

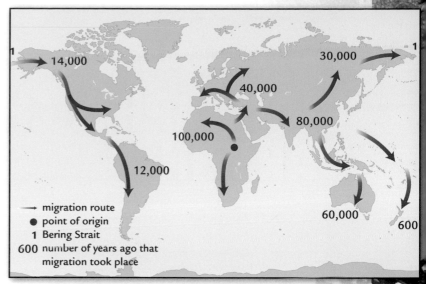

Following the Herto finds, scientists are now sure that all modern humans descend from people who lived in Africa around 100,000 years ago. Their descendants included migrants who, by 12,000 years ago, had colonized all the major nonpolar landmasses in the world.

hunting, these people became farmers, and the first towns developed. More advances swiftly followed, including the development of writing. Civilization as we know it had begun.

ARE HUMANS STILL EVOLVING?

People often think of human evolution as a finished process ending with us. But like other species, humans are still evolving. As people lead less active lives, humans may lose some of their muscles. On the other hand, improved diet may make future generations taller. In recent years harmful ultraviolet radiation from the sun has reached Earth owing to ozone loss in the atmosphere. This radiation causes skin damage, particularly in fair-skinned people. Natural selection may favor darker-skinned people, who are less at risk.

CHAPTER NINE

BIOGRAPHY: CHARLES DARWIN

Charles Darwin was born in Shrewsbury, in the west of England, on February 12, 1809, to a talented family. Notable members include Charles's grandfather, Erasmus Darwin, a scientist, poet, and a leading physician.

In 1818, Charles started at Shrewsbury School, where his interest in science soon became evident. In 1825 he went to the University of Edinburgh to study medicine, which, despite being the son and grandson of doctors, he hated. Darwin left Edinburgh in 1828 without taking a degree, and enrolled at Christ's College, Cambridge, to study theology. Once again, he found he was not greatly interested in the main subject of his studies, but took the opportunity to develop his interest in scientific pursuits by joining a number of natural history societies. He got to know several eminent scientists

This portrait of Charles Darwin was painted by artist John Collier.

KEY DATES

1809	Born on February 12 in Shrewsbury, England
1825–28	Studies medicine at Edinburgh University
1828	Enters Christ's College, Cambridge, England, to study theology
1831	Appointed naturalist on HMS *Beagle*
1832–36	Travels in and around South America on *Beagle*
1839	Marries his cousin Emma Wedgwood in January; publishes *Journal of Researches into the Geology and Natural History of the Various Countries Visited by HMS Beagle...*
1842	Writes first, 35-page, draft of his evolutionary theory
1858	On June 18 receives an essay from naturalist Alfred Russel Wallace outlining Wallace's theory of natural selection; Darwin and Wallace present joint paper to the Linnean Society in London on July 1
1859	*On the Origin of Species by Means of Natural Selection* published on November 26
1871	Publication of *The Descent of Man, and Selection in Relation to Sex*
1882	Dies from heart attack on April 19; buried in Westminster Abbey

at Cambridge, including John Stevens Henslow, professor of botany, and Adam Sedgwick, professor of geology. In the summer of 1831 Darwin accompanied Sedgwick on a three-week field excursion to Wales during which he received his only formal scientific training.

A PROMISING OPPORTUNITY

In London, Robert Fitzroy, captain of HMS *Beagle*, was preparing an expedition to survey the coasts of South America for the Royal Navy. He asked the naval authorities to advertise for "some well-educated and scientific person" to be part of the voyage.

Henslow advised Darwin to apply, and on September 5, 1831, Darwin traveled to meet Fitzroy. They got on very well, and on December 27 the *Beagle* sailed from Portsmouth with Charles on board.

HOW GEOLOGY SHAPED THE WORLD

Until the 18th century, people believed that the Earth had been created literally as described in the Bible, that it was a few thousand rather than millions of years old, and that it had been shaped by violent events controlled by God. However, some scientists, including Scottish scientist James Hutton, began to speculate that the Earth's history was much longer than had previously been supposed. Hutton suggested that the Earth had changed very slowly over millions of years, and that it was still changing. Apart from directly challenging the literal biblical version of events, this theory led to the creation of a new science, geology, which was the study of the origin, history, structure, and makeup of the Earth.

By the early 19th century Scottish geologist Charles Lyell had reached the same conclusion as Hutton. Lyell and his supporters became known as the "uniformitarians," because of their theory that geological features changed regularly or "uniformly." This explained why rivers eroded valleys and the sea wore away cliffs. Hutton and Lyell's theories met with strong resistance for many years.

Darwin read Lyell's book and was greatly impressed by it. What Darwin saw over the months and years of the *Beagle*'s trip soon persuaded him that Lyell's theories were correct.

THE INHERITANCE OF ACQUIRED CHARACTERISTICS

In the same way that Christians believed the biblical account of the age of the Earth, they also believed that God had created animals and plants and that species did not change. By the end of the 18th century, however, some people were questioning these views.

Distinguished French naturalist the Chevalier de Lamarck (Jean Baptiste Pierre Antoine de Monet) suggested that, over many generations, the frequent use of an organ by a species would gradually enlarge and strengthen it; lack of use would diminish and weaken it until it disappeared, and that these changes, through use or disuse, would be passed on to offspring. For example, he thought that the neck of a giraffe would lengthen as it stretched for leaves on high trees, and that the next generation would inherit this "long-neckedness." His theory is now called "Lamarckism" or "the inheritance of acquired characteristics." No instance of it has ever been found. Although Darwin's own theory was superficially similar to Lamarck's, it contains some very significant differences, and was developed from the actual observations Darwin made during his voyage.

SETTING OUT

In December 1831 the *Beagle* left port. When the *Beagle* made its first landfall at Saint Jago in the Cape Verde Islands, off the coast of West Africa, Darwin was thrilled at his first sight of a volcanic island. The island's rock strata provided him with evidence to support the idea of slow change described in Lyell's book. He found a layer of limestone rock nearly 45 feet (14m) above sea level that contained seashells; similar material was forming by the seashore. Clearly, either the sea was once much higher, or the land was once lower.

From here the *Beagle* crossed the Atlantic to Brazil, eventually landing at Rio de Janeiro on April 4, 1832. Darwin was transfixed by everything he saw. He collected hundreds of specimens, which he sent home to Henslow.

Next the *Beagle* set sail for the remote lands of Patagonia and Tierra del Fuego. At Punta Alta, on the shores of Patagonia, Darwin found a cliff made up of shingle, gravel, and a layer of red clay. In this he discovered some enormous bones, which he realized must have belonged to creatures far bigger than any now in existence. These were the remains of giant sloths (Megatherium and Megalonyx), giant armadillos (Myelodon and Glyptodon), and Macrauchenia, an animal that resembled a camel, but with claws. He saw that they resembled similar modern, much smaller species, and wondered why the giant species had become extinct.

DESTRUCTION AND DISCOVERY

By early 1834 the *Beagle* was heading back to the Pacific through terrible

This lithograph of two ground finches from the Galápagos Islands by Elizabeth Gould was based on a drawing by her husband, English ornithologist, John Gould.

storms. On July 22, 1834 it reached Valparaíso, in Chile. Darwin set off to explore the Andes. When he found fossil seashells at 12,000 feet (3658m), it confirmed the picture that had been forming in his mind: this part of South America must once have lain beneath the sea, and later been pushed back up above sea level. The mountains would first have appeared as islands in the sea, and eventually been raised further to form mountain chains.

On February 20, 1835, a severe earthquake in Chile destroyed the city of Concepción. Darwin, who had been working at Valdivia, south of Concepción, noticed that the level of the land had risen after the earthquake, and that a new island had emerged in the ocean close to the island group of Juan Fernández. To Darwin this was proof of his theory that land could rise up from the sea and eventually form mountain ranges.

In September 1835 the *Beagle* arrived in the Galápagos Islands, home to several varieties of finches. Darwin collected as many specimens as he could, studying them more closely only after his return to England.

A GROWING REPUTATION

On October 2, 1836, a year after its visit to the Galápagos Islands, the *Beagle* arrived back in Portsmouth, southern England. Some of Darwin's geological reports had been published in journals while he was away, and he returned to find himself already recognized as a leading scientific figure. Charles Lyell was greatly impressed by Darwin's work, and he became a personal friend.

Darwin went first to Cambridge, where he and Henslow began sorting out the many specimens that Darwin had brought back. They also started to prepare Darwin's record of the voyage, which was published in 1839.

DEVELOPING A THEORY OF EVOLUTION

In 1837 Darwin moved to London, the same year he began work on the first of the many notebooks in which he gathered information about species.

In June 1842, Darwin wrote a first draft of what would become his theory of evolution by natural selection. Evolution is the gradual change in the characteristics of plants and animals over successive generations. Two years later Darwin wrote a much longer second draft. His attention then turned to revising the *Journal* for its second edition, and when that was done he wrote another book. Darwin then spent several years studying barnacles. All the time, though, he continued to collect information about species and discuss his developing ideas with others. In 1856 he started to write what he considered the most complete statement of his ideas. However, Darwin only made a few friends aware of the work he was doing, and he was not yet ready to publish it.

TWO MEN, ONE THEORY

Darwin had written about half of the book by the middle of 1858, when on June 18 he received an essay written by the Welsh naturalist Alfred Russel Wallace. The two men had corresponded before, and Darwin realized that Wallace had reached exactly the same conclusion as he had about the way species evolve. Both men had found that, within each species, some individuals have a characteristic (variation) that makes their survival more likely. They pass this feature on to their offspring, and gradually each generation that follows becomes more and more adapted to its particular environment. This was the theory of natural selection that Darwin worked out from his study of the Galápagos finches.

Although Darwin had formed his theory years earlier, a "joint paper" was presented to the Linnean Society in London on July 1, 1858. Neither Darwin nor Wallace was present, however, and the paper aroused very little interest.

Darwin's idea had been to publish his theory as a series of papers submitted to the society, but there proved to be too much material to make this practical. Instead, he prepared a popular, shortened account of his theory and published it in the form of a book called *On the Origin of Species by Means of Natural Selection, or The Preservation of Favoured Races in the Struggle for Life*. The first edition of 1,250 copies, published on November 26, 1859, sold out on the first day.

Darwin readily admitted that his theory presented difficulties. In particular, he had no idea how variation could emerge within a species or how characters could be inherited. He suggested the environment might stimulate variation, rather in the way proposed by Lamarck.

THE DARWIN-WALLACE THEORY

When scientists speak of "the theory of evolution," the theory they have in mind is the one that was put forward by Darwin and Wallace, in which natural selection is the mechanism that drives forward the evolution of species. Evolution itself is not a theory, it is a fact, and one that has been observed happening many times. It is the descent of organisms from generation to generation with slight modification until they are so different from their ancestors that they make up a new species.

The Darwinian (or Darwin-Wallace) theory proceeds in seven steps. 1. Individuals resemble their parents. 2. The individuals belonging to a species are slightly different from one another. 3. Members of each generation usually produce more offspring than are needed to replace their parents. 4. Despite this, populations tend to remain stable and it is clearly impossible for a population to increase in size indefinitely. 5. Since populations remain stable, not all offspring can survive; therefore there must be competition to survive among the offspring. 6. The survivors will be

RELIGION AND SCIENCE

The publication of Darwin's *On the Origin of Species* struck at the heart of religious belief in a fundamental manner. It challenged religious thinking in two ways: by questioning the literal truth of the biblical description of the Creation, and by undermining the idea that humans were unique, and different from animals.

Christians believed that mankind had been created by God "in His image." In *Descent of Man*, Darwin wrote that mankind "is descended from some lowly organized form," and that "there is no fundamental difference between man and higher animals in their mental faculties." To many people, therefore, Darwin's ideas amounted to a direct attack on the word of God.

In June 1860 a debate took place between an opponent of Darwin's theory, the bishop of Winchester, Samuel Wilberforce, and one of Darwin's supporters, the English biologist Thomas Henry Huxley. The bishop began by mocking Darwin's theory of evolution, saying that it went against the word of the Bible. He then asked Huxley sarcastically whether he was descended from an ape on his grandfather's or his grandmother's side. Huxley was furious. As the audience listened in amazement, Huxley robustly stated that he would rather have an ape for a grandfather than a man such as the bishop.

A contemporary sketch shows Bishop Samuel Wilberforce, who attacked Darwin's theories for going against religious beliefs.

those individuals who differ from their fellows in ways that allow them to use the resources available to them more efficiently. 7. Environmental conditions change over long periods of time, as Lyell had shown. These changes naturally select the variations within a species that are best suited to them; the changes also encourage new variations to emerge. Eventually the variations are so marked that a completely new species is formed, so it is natural selection, through changing environmental conditions, that causes new species to emerge.

LATER LIFE

Charles Darwin was a gentle, modest man, who held liberal views on social matters. He married his first cousin Emma Wedgwood in 1839 and the couple had 10 children. Although misinterpretation of his ideas, deliberate or otherwise, made Darwin the subject of ridicule and anger, he continued to develop his theory, discussing human origins in *The Descent of Man, and Selection in Relation to Sex* (1871). For most of his life, he suffered from intermittent symptoms of sickness that made him a semi-invalid; no one is quite sure of the cause. Darwin died on April 19, 1882, and was buried in Westminster Abbey, London.

SCIENTIFIC BACKGROUND

Before 1820

Scottish scientist James Hutton (1725–1797) argues that the Earth is millions of years old

Darwin's grandfather, Erasmus Darwin (1731–1802), suggests that species might be transformable

French naturalist the Chevalier de Lamarck (1744–1829) proposes that species can inherit characteristics acquired by the previous generation

English clergyman Thomas Malthus (1766–1834) writes an *Essay on Population* in which he maintains that a struggle for survival in populations is inevitable

1820

1820–40 English geologists William Buckland (1784–1836) and Adam Sedgwick (1785–1873) develop their "catastrophist" view of geological history

1827 French mathematician Jean Baptiste Fourier (1768–1830) suggests that human activities have an effect on the Earth's climate

1830

1831 Darwin sets sail with Captain Robert Fitzroy on HMS *Beagle* as the expedition's unpaid naturalist

1835 Darwin makes important discoveries about the evolution of species on the Galápagos Islands

1839 Darwin publishes his *Journal of Researches into the Geology and Natural History of the Various Countries Visited by HMS* Beagle

1837 Darwin reads Thomas Malthus's *Essay on Population*

1840

1842 Darwin writes the first draft of his theory of evolution

1844 Robert Chambers (1802–1871) publishes anonymously his theory of the development of species in *Vestiges of Creation*

1848–52 Welsh botanist Alfred Russel Wallace (1823–1913) collects specimens in South America

POLITICAL AND CULTURAL BACKGROUND

1815 After his defeat at the Battle of Waterloo, French emperor Napoleon Bonaparte (1769–1821) throws himself on the mercy of the British but is banished to the island of Saint Helena in the south Atlantic Ocean

1824 German composer Ludwig van Beethoven (1770–1827) completes his *Mass in D Major*

1826 American novelist James Fenimore Cooper (1789–1851) publishes *The Last of the Mohicans,* one of a series of novels by Cooper that take pioneer and American Indian life as their subject

1827 *An American Dictionary of the English Language* is published after 28 years of work by American lexicographer Noah Webster (1758–1843)

1837 American inventor Samuel Finley Breese Morse (1791–1872) patents his version of the telegraph, a machine that sends letters in code

1837 In Britain, Queen Victoria (1819–1901) comes to the throne. She will rule for the rest of the 19th century, and until her death in 1901

1844 American inventor Charles Goodyear (1800–60) treats rubber with sulfur under heat and pressure to make it more elastic and strong; the process, known as "vulcanizing," allows the development of the rubber tires for which he becomes famous

1846 Famine sweeps Ireland as the potato crop fails

1850

1854–62 Wallace travels to the Malay archipelago and the East Indies (now Indonesia), and collects more than 125,000 specimens

1858 Darwin and Wallace present a joint paper on their theory of natural selection to the Linnean Society in London; in 1859 Darwin publishes *On the Origin of Species by Natural Selection*

1858 Wallace reads Malthus's *Essay on Population* and forms theory of "survival of the fittest," which he sends to Darwin

1860

1863 British geologist Charles Lyell (1797–1875) and British zoologist Thomas Huxley (1825–1895) publish *Antiquity of Man* and *Man's Place in Nature*

1865 Austrian botanist Gregor Mendel (1822–1884) publishes his theory of a law of inheritance, but it does not gain much attention until 1900

1869–1910 Darwin's cousin Francis Galton (1822–1911) develops eugenics, the breeding of human beings for evolutionary improvement

1870

1871 Darwin's work *The Descent of Man* concludes that man evolved from apelike ancestors in Africa

1871 A prehistoric pterodactyl skeleton is identified by the first American paleontologist, Othniel Charles Marsh (1831–1899)

1880 French chemist Louis Pasteur (1822–1895) develops the germ theory of disease

1880

1887 Belgian cytologist Eduard van Beneden (1817–1910) discovers that each species has a fixed number of chromosomes

1889 Wallace publishes *Darwinism* and receives the first Darwin Medal

1890

After 1890

1890–96 "Lamarckism" rejected by German biologist August Weismann (1834–1919)

1900 Mendel's theory of inheritance is revived

1902 American geneticist Walter Stanborough Sutton (1877–1916) states that chromosomes are paired and may be the carriers of heredity

1850 German chemist and physicist Robert Wilhelm Bunsen (1811–1899) invents the Bunsen burner

1850 Bavarian-American entrepreneur Levi Strauss (1829–1902) introduces "bibless overalls," the forerunner of denim jeans, for miners in California

1859 American landscape painter Frederick E. Church (1826–1900) completes *Heart of the Andes*

1867 German social, political, and economic theorist Karl Marx (1818–1883) publishes *Das Kapital*, in which he develops the theory of the evolution of society

1865 The American Civil War ends, President Lincoln is assassinated, and a 12-year "Era of Reconstruction" begins in the South

1870 The Vatican Council votes that the pope is infallible when defining doctrines of faith or morals

1877 The disputed 1876 election for the U.S. presidency is resolved when an electoral committee declares in favor of the Republican Rutherford B. Hayes (1822–1893)

1884 American writer Mark Twain (1835–1910) publishes *The Adventures of Huckleberry Finn*. The author takes his pen-name from the phrase used by men testing depths in shallow rivers: "mark twain" means that the mark shows the river is two fathoms deep

1886 In the United States, Coca-Cola goes on sale for the first time. Made by an Atlanta chemist, its ingredients include South American coca and African kola nuts

1893 A four-year economic depression begins in the United States. On June 27 the Wall Street stock market collapses as share prices plummet

allele Any of the alternative forms of a gene that may occur at a given point on a chromosome.

allopatric speciation The formation of new species through geographic isolation.

anatomy Structural makeup of an organism.

antibiotic Drug that kills bacteria.

artificial selection Change over time of domesticated organisms due to selection (breeding) by people.

asexual reproduction Production of young without the need for mating or the fusion of sex cells.

biogeography The study of where organisms live and how they got there.

biological arms race The coevolution of predators and their prey.

chromosome Structure in the nucleus that contains DNA.

classification The organization of different organisms into related groups by biologists.

coevolution Evolution involving changes in two species that depend on each other to survive.

convergent evolution When distantly related creatures evolve similar body plans in response to similar environments.

creationism Theory that organisms were created by God and do not evolve.

cryptic species Species that is indistinguishable from another without genetic study.

deoxyribonucleic acid (DNA) Molecule that contains the genetic code for all cellular (nonvirus) organisms.

endemic Organism that lives in just one place, typically an island.

eukaryote Cell containing organelles; animals, plants, and fungi are eukaryotes.

evolution Process of change in groups of organisms over long periods of time.

extinct When the last individual of a species dies.

fertilization The fusion of a sperm with an egg.

fitness The relative ability of an organism to survive and produce viable young.

fossil The remains or traces of long-dead organisms replaced by minerals.

founder effect Phenomenon that causes low genetic diversity and unusual genes to be expressed in populations (such as those on islands) founded by just a few individuals.

gene Section of DNA that codes for the structure of a protein.

gene flow Passage of genes through a geographically linked population.

gene pool The total variation of genes in a population.

genetic bottleneck Loss of genetic diversity caused by very low population levels.

genetic drift The random loss of genetic diversity; especially important in small populations or ones on islands.

geologist Scientist who studies rocks.

hominid Member of the family Hominidae, to which people belong.

hybrid Young produced by breeding between individuals of different species.

inbreeding depression Lack of fitness due to inbreeding, caused by a buildup of recessive genes.

iterative evolution Repeated evolution of similar structures in different groups over long periods of time.

Lamarckism Outdated evolutionary theory that suggested that a parent's features changed according to use during its lifetime before being inherited by young.

mass extinction A relatively swift die-off of large numbers of species.

meiosis Cell division that leads to the production of sex cells.

melanistic When an individual is much darker than normal, such as in panthers.

minimum viable population The smallest possible population a species can tolerate before extinction becomes inevitable.

mutation A change to a gene; can be neutral (have no effect), negative, or positive.

natural selection Theory that only the fittest organisms survive and reproduce; one of the causes of evolution.

neo-Darwinism Branch of evolutionary theory that incorporates natural selection with advances in the understanding of genetics.

niche The ecological role of an organism in an ecosystem.

paleontologist Scientist who studies fossils.

polyploid Organism with extra sets of chromosomes.

predator Animal that catches other animals for food.

prokaryote Single-celled organism, such as a bacterium, that does not contain miniorgans.

punctuated equilibrium Theory that rapid bursts of evolutionary change are separated by much longer periods of little change.

recombination The shuffling of genes during sexual reproduction. It leads to increased genetic diversity.

reproductive isolation The separation of one population from another so they cannot interbreed.

sexual dimorphism Anatomical differences between males and females of the same species.

sexual reproduction Production of young through the fusion of sex cells, often after mating between a male and a female.

sexual selection Form of natural selection driven by an organism's preference for characteristics in a mate.

species A group of organisms that can potentially mate with each other to produce young that can also interbreed successfully.

spontaneous generation Ancient belief that organisms could arise directly from nonliving matter.

subspecies Subdivision of a species; a population that may have different colorings and a different range than other subspecies but can still interbreed with them.

sympatric speciation The formation of new species through behavioral and other mechanisms rather than geographic isolation.

vertebrate Animal with a backbone.

vestigial structure An organ or structure that has become redundant, or may be used for a completely different purpose than its original function.

zygote An egg fertilized by a sperm that will develop into a new organism.

Canadian Institute of Ecology and
Evolution
3737 Wascana Pkwy.
University of Regina
Regina, SK S4S 0A2
Canada
(306) 337-8867
Web site: http://ciee-icee.com
The Canadian Institute of Ecology and
Evolution, a consortium of research
universities from throughout Canada,
seeks to bring together and train new
generations of scientists represent-
ing various research areas with the
aim of finding insights and solutions
for critical environmental issues.

Down House
Luxted Road
Downe, Kent
London Borough of Bromley
England BR6 7JT
0 1689 859119
Web site: http://www.english-heritage
.org.uk/daysout/properties/home
-of-charles-dawin-down-house
Down House was the home of Charles
Darwin and is now open to the pub-
lic for tours, lectures, and more.

National Center for Science Education
420 40th Street Suite 2
Oakland, CA 94609
(510) 601-7203
Web site: http://ncse.com
The National Center for Science
Education offers information and
resources to schools and members

of the public interested in promoting the teaching of evolution in the
classroom.

National Evolutionary Synthesis Center
2024 W. Main Street
Suite A200
Durham, NC 27705
(919) 668-4551
Web site: http://www.nescent.org
By promoting cross-disciplinary research,
the National Evolutionary Synthesis
Center seeks to ask and answer
significant questions related to evolution. Its Education and Outreach
group works with the public to com-
municate the center's goals and to
improve evolution education.

National Museum of Natural History
Smithsonian Institution
P.O. Box 37012
Washington, DC 20013
(202) 633-1000
Web site: http://www.mnh.si.edu
The exhibits at the National Museum of
Natural History survey the world's
history, cultures, and biodiversity
through its exhibits, collections, and
research. Among its many attrac-
tions is FossiLab, which allows
visitors to watch paleontologists
at work, and the Hall of Human
Origins, which chronicles the evolution of humans.

Royal Tyrell Museum
Highway 838 Midland Provincial Park

Drumheller, Alberta T0J 0Y0
Canada
(888) 440-4240
Web site: http://www.tyrrellmuseum.com
The Royal Tyrell Museum is dedicated
    to inspiring interest in the science of
    paleontology through its collections,
    research, and outreach programs.
    Its many exhibits include one of the
    world's largest displays of dinosaurs.

Society for the Study of Evolution
4475 Castleman Avenue
St. Louis, MO 63110
(314) 577-9554
Web site: http://www.evolutionsociety.org
The Society for the Study of Evolution
    seeks to promote the study of

evolution by holding annual meet-
ings for findings in evolutionary
biology to be shared and discussed
as well as various education
and outreach initiatives. It also
publishes the scientific journal
Evolution.

WEB SITES

Due to the changing nature of Internet
links, Rosen Publishing has developed
an online list of Web sites related to the
subject of this book. This site is updated
regularly. Please use this link to access
the list:

http://www.rosenlinks.com/CORE/Evol

Ackroyd, Peter. *The Beginning*. London, UK: Dorling Kindersley, 2003.

Dawkins, Richard. *The Greatest Show on Earth: The Evidence for Evolution*. New York, NY: Free Press, 2009.

Day, Trevor. *Routes of Science: Genetics*. San Diego, CA: Blackbirch Press, 2004.

Gates, Phil. *Horrible Science: Evolve or Die*. New York, NY: Scholastic, 1999.

Gould, Stephen Jay. *Wonderful Life: The Burgess Shale and the Nature of History*. New York, NY: W.W. Norton, 1989.

Howard, Jonathan. *Darwin: A Very Short Introduction*. New York, NY: Oxford University Press, 2001.

Mayr, Ernst. *What Evolution Is*. New York, NY: BasicBooks, 2001.

Milner, Richard. *Darwin's Universe: Evolution from A to Z*. Berkeley, CA: University of California Press, 2009.

Olson, Steve. *Mapping Human History: Discovering the Past Through Our Genes*. Boston, MA: Houghton Mifflin Co., 2002.

Quammen, David. *The Reluctant Mr. Darwin: An Intimate Portrait of Charles Darwin and the Making of His Theory of Evolution*. New York, NY: Atlas, 2007.

Roberts, Alice. *Evolution: The Human Story*. New York, NY: DK Publishing, 2011.

Ward, David, and Cyril Walker. *DK Handbook: Fossils*. New Yor, NYk: DK Publishing, 2000.

Zimmer, Carl. *Evolution: The Triumph of an Idea*. New York, NY: HarperCollins, 2006.

PHOTO CREDITS